IRELAND'S
INVASION
OF THE WORLD

IRELAND'S INVASION OF THE WORLD

OF THE WORLD

THE IRISH DIASPORA IN A NUTSHELL

MIKI GARCIA

First published 2015

The History Press Ireland
50 City Quay
Dublin 2
Ireland
www.thehistorypress.ie

British Library Cataloguing in Publication Data.
A catalogue record for this book is available from the British Library.

ISBN 978 1 84588 834 3

Typesetting and origination by The History Press

CONTENTS

INTRODUCTION

Ireland is complicated. So are its people.

For a start, the island of Ireland is not a united country. There is a border that divides the Republic of Ireland and the six counties of Ulster which still belong to the United Kingdom. In Northern Ireland, some people carry Irish passports and call themselves Irish while others profess their loyalty to the British Crown, call themselves British and carry British passports. And there are some who carry both. In earlier times, a small minority of Anglo-Irish Protestants refused to call themselves Irish. They considered themselves part of a privileged social class and didn't want to be associated with Catholic Irish people.

So who are the Irish exactly? Defining national identity can be a serious issue in today's genetically, politically and socially mixed Ireland. Many Irish national heroes, or those who died or lived for Ireland, were not in fact Irish at all, or at least were not actually born or bred on the island of Ireland. Many of them were immigrants themselves. For instance, James Connolly was from Scotland, Éamon de Valera was born in New York to a Spanish father, Charles Stewart Parnell's mother was American, Maud Gonne was English, Countess Markievicz was born Constance Georgine Gore-Booth in London. Needless to say, they are only the tip of the iceberg. The past struggles of many hitherto unacclaimed people in Ireland and abroad have contributed immensely to creating the present reality in Ireland. In the words of Irish nationalist Thomas Davis, 'It is not blood that makes you Irish but a willingness to be part of the Irish nation.'

Many assume the Irish were a Celtic race. The Celts certainly arrived in Ireland and the Irish are culturally Celtic, but the people who put down roots on the island of Ireland came from all over the place and have more complex origins. During the last ice age, hunter-gatherers from Britain and Europe – most notably from the Basque region straddling modern-day Spain and France – arrived on these shores. One of the oldest books in Ireland, called the *Leabhar* Gabhála (the Book of Invasions), talks about an invasion by the Celtic King Milesius and the settlers he brought with him, who were a small, dark people from Spain. With a tendency to follow leaders, these tribes were known to be poetic and warlike. Later, various newcomers from other European countries arrived – Vikings, Normans, English, Romans, Scottish, Huguenots, Palatines, Dutch, Belgians, Jews and many more to follow. Gradually, they all blended in with the existing groups, adopting the society's social values, and pagan people gradually became mainly Catholic and Irish in terms of psychology and behaviour.

In its more recent history, Ireland has been defined by emigration and its large diaspora. According to the *Oxford English Dictionary*, the word 'diaspora' means 'the dispersion or spread of any people from their original homeland'. The Irish diaspora is the largest in the world, exceeding that of the Greeks and the Jews. It is estimated that there are over 100 million people with Irish ancestors worldwide while the population of the whole of Ireland was just over 6 million in 2013. The catastrophic potato famine, known as the Great Hunger or *An Gorta Mór*, which occurred in 1845, was a turning point in Irish history. Emigration became a *leitmotif* and by the turn of the twentieth century, about a third of all people born in Ireland were living elsewhere.

But it wasn't only during the famine years that the Irish left the country in large numbers. In fact, they had been emigrating for centuries, and have gained a reputation for being constantly on the move, leading to the occasional quip about 'the wandering Irish'. The Irish diaspora has had an immeasurable impact on the shaping of Ireland and Irish national identity, but it has also hugely influenced the cultures and politics of the countries around the world with a strong Irish presence.

For such a tiny island, located at the westernmost edge of Europe, Ireland has always punched above its weight and its inhabitants can be considered one of the great pioneering races. During medieval times, Irish monks travelled extensively to European countries and helped civilise barbarian Europe. In later years, the Scots-Irish immigrants helped shape the cultural and political ideas in the US and consequently their American Republican ideas were brought back to Ireland. Daniel O'Connell shaped the concept of civil rights, which was conveyed by immigrants to others in their adoptive lands all across the globe. Irish missionaries also had a considerable influence in the receiving societies, particularly in the field of education.

The historical connections between Britain and Ireland meant that the Irish scattered to all corners of the world with the spread of the British Empire which, at its height, ruled over more than a quarter of the world's population. Wherever there was a British presence, the Irish could also be found. Although the majority of them became part of the Irish diaspora as forced or involuntary immigrants, a large number of them were active participants in British expansionism. The fact that they did not have their own empire does not imply that they were not also invaders.

It is not easy, however, to ascertain the number of Irish emigrants abroad. As a coloniser, England was supposed to know what their people were up to. Not only did the English – normally meticulous record keepers – forget to jot down details of Irish emigrants when they were leaving, but some host countries also got confused about how to categorise Irish immigrants as long-term British subjects could be classified as English, Scottish or British. Irish citizenship didn't exist until the twentieth century, so they often had to declare themselves as English when abroad or the local authorities assumed they were indeed English. For instance, during the California Gold Rush, many foreign consulates had hastily opened when would-be gold miners packed like sardines into the insignificant fishing village of San Francisco. By 1853, at least twenty-seven foreign consulates were actively dealing with their country's citizens. Among the most numerous immigrants were the Irish, who were typically travelling as British subjects.

Many Irish immigrants arrived in their new countries destitute, but they fought for their adoptive country as soldiers and commanders, served as indentured labourers on plantations, built railroads, roads and canals, looked after privileged people as domestic servants, and dug for silver and gold in the mines. Others rose to become millionaires, influential politicians, and highly skilled professionals. Some Irish immigrants were well accepted in certain localities, particularly Irish Catholic missionaries and nuns. They were often the most efficient immigrants, especially in nascent countries, as they didn't just spread Catholicism, build churches and look after the unfortunate but also established academic institutions, schools and hospitals, and taught both Catholics and non-Catholics alike, wherever they were needed. These pioneering educators and medical professionals played a crucial role in the development of dozens of nations. Not to mention the fact that in wartime they often tended the sick or soldiers on far-flung battlefields, sometimes even travelling with them.

As they moved from place to place, involuntarily or voluntarily, with myriad reasons many quickly assimilated into their adoptive countries and formed new identities, others became more Irish abroad, creating Irish communities, celebrating and spreading their culture. As a result, today Irish festivals are celebrated far and wide. Originally the Celtic festival of Samhain, or summer's end, Halloween served to mark the end of the harvest season and the beginning of the 'darker half' of the year. There is also the self-explanatory St Patrick's Day celebrations on 17 March, which is a date on which people worldwide celebrate all things Irish and everyone can think of themselves as Irish, regardless of their religious belief, ethnicity or the passport they carry. Consequently, the omnipresence of Irish pubs all across the world is more palpable than the presence of Irish embassies. Nowadays Bloomsday on 16 June is rapidly catching up with this global trend, particularly for those of a literary bent. The day is a celebration of the Irish writer James Joyce. The name is derived from Leopold Bloom, the protagonist of Joyce's internationally famous novel *Ulysses*. The action of the novel takes place on 16 June, but it was also the date on which Joyce went out with Nora Barnacle – his future wife – for the first time.

Whether they were fighting, building burgeoning nations, benefiting from the war industries or famine economies, countless Irish immigrants became part of the various histories of the countries mentioned in this book. As a group they became one of the most influential groups of people in the course of human history.

I hope you will find out more about this fascinating aspect of Ireland and her people in the pages of this little book.

1

BRITAIN

Ever since the Norman invasion of Ireland in 1169, Ireland has been inseparably involved with Britain politically, economically and socially. Edward I, King of England declared that 'Ireland shall never be separated from the crown of England'.

Although it was not until the seventeenth century that England officially took control of the island of Ireland, the movement of people and goods between Ireland and mainland Britain had been happening for centuries.

Taking the boat and crossing the Irish Sea to Britain has long been considered a sensible thing to do when times are bad back home. Many Irish traditionally worked as seasonal harvest workers or temporary workers and came home on a regular basis. However, others found permanent jobs, started families and settled down in Britain.

It is estimated that more than 10 per cent of the British population has some kind of Irish connection and for many years the Irish were the largest minority group in England. However, many felt that they remained in a 'curious middle place', being neither completely Irish nor British.

One cannot easily distinguish Irish contributions to Britain because the Irish are very much part of it: many English, Scottish and Welsh people have Irish ancestors and visa versa and they also share much of the same history and culture. Historically, the relationships between Scotland, Wales, England and Ireland have been reciprocal.

Ireland is a melting pot of people after all – Irish people all initially came from somewhere else, be it as invaders, colonisers, refugees, fugitives, adventurers, ordinary settlers and so on. When the early Vikings who had settled in Ireland were kicked out of Ireland, they ended up emigrating to England. Ireland invaded Wales and Welsh people had also been settling in Ireland. Scotland and Ireland both have Gaelic languages and share many aspects of Gaelic culture.

Although the Irish have been continuously emigrating to Britain, the major turning point was the Great Famine of 1845-49, when an unprecedented number of them arrived on British shores. It is estimated that 1 million Irish died and another 1 million emigrated to various countries during the crisis.

The Irish history of oppression and resistance meant many Irish migrants strove to achieve fairness in their new country. As capable team players and persistent organisers, trade unions in Britain and elsewhere often consisted of large numbers of Irish immigrants and descendants.

The establishment of the Irish Free State in 1922 didn't change much. During this period of political turmoil there was a continuous flow of immigrants and a huge wave of people arrived at the post-war period of the 1950s. Many of these migrants went on to work in the National Health Service (NHS) hospitals or in infrastructure projects, helping to rebuild and reshape Britain that had been ravaged by the war. After this period, the next big emigration peak came in the 1980s. These were very different immigrants from previous waves: these immigrants were highly skilled workers with university degrees or other professional qualifications who were not able to find a job in their chosen fields in their own country.

SCOTLAND

The DNA of Scottish and Irish people are extremely similar, suggesting that they are all descended from the same stock. Many early settlers in Scotland were originally from Ireland, or de facto invaders, and Scottish people also emigrated to Ireland. Both groups ultimately helped shape Irish and Scottish identities. Although both

Scotland and Ireland had invaded and rebelled against one another in the past, they naturally influenced each other in countless ways until the serious political factor kicked in: the plantation of Ulster, which began in the seventeenth century when Scottish and English Protestants settled in Ulster. This single event resulted in bloody revolts and suppressions for centuries to come.

One of the famous early emigrants to Scotland was St Columba (521-597). Born into the O'Donnell clan in Garten, County Donegal, he showed a strong interest in the Church as a teenager. As a missionary, he established various monasteries in Ireland as well as the church of Derry and went on to spread Christianity all across Scotland, most famously founding the abbey on Iona.

Traditionally, Irish people crossed the sea to Scotland during the agricultural planting and harvest season and by the 1850s, up to 60,000 Irish harvest workers were recorded in Scotland. Those temporary workers didn't form permanent settlements but they did enhance the tie between the two countries. It was industrialisation that gave them reasons to stay, when stable job opportunities in the cotton-weaving and railway industries became available, allowing them to permanently leave behind the political and economic problems on Irish soil. There was simply not enough industry in Ireland to cater to all those looking for work; although Belfast, the biggest city in Ireland at the time, was relatively developed and industrialised.

Eventually large Irish communities on the west coast of Scotland, such as Wigtownshire and Kirkcudbrightshire, became visible. Due to the wide range of job opportunities in industrial areas such as Glasgow, Irish immigrants steadily arrived in droves and by 1851 nearly 30 per cent of the population in Glasgow was from Ireland. And it wasn't just in Glasgow that the Irish settled; Irish dock workers could be found everywhere on the Scottish coast and nearly 50 per cent of female textile workers in Greenock in 1851 were Irish immigrants.

In the late nineteenth century, however, the wave of Catholic immigration dwindled to a trickle. Instead, Protestant Irish people from Ulster came to represent the majority of newcomers. Scottish Orangeism originated from the Irish Rebellion of 1798, when Scottish soldiers from fencible regiments were sent to Ireland to fight the rebellion. Established in 1800, the Orange

Order is the biggest and oldest Protestant fraternity institution in Scotland. It is a Protestant fraternal organisation which was founded in 1796 in Belfast, Northern Ireland. It was named after the Dutch-born Protestant King William of Orange, who defeated the Catholic King James II during the Battle of the Boyne, which took place near Drogheda, Ireland, in 1690. To promote Protestant civil and religious liberties, the organisation has branches in the Commonwealth countries and the US. With the hordes of new settlers, it gained more power and influence in Scotland. Sectarianism has always been present but the Irish assimilated into Scottish society much more smoothly and with less hassle than in other parts of Britain.

The Irish started building their own settlements and soon became self-sufficient. The majority of them were able to find marriage partners of Irish extraction but most of the time children born to Irish parents became Scottish and spoke English with a Scottish accent.

One of the most well-known Irish person that Scotland has produced is James Connolly (1868-1916). The Irish republican and socialist leader was born in the Cowgate area, which was also known as the 'Irish Slum' or 'Little Ireland', of Edinburgh to Irish parents from County Monaghan. Life as immigrants in Scotland could be just as harsh and unfulfilling as life in Ireland and Connolly's mother died early as a result of their impoverished lifestyle. He joined the British Army as a teenager and was stationed in County Cork, where he witnessed social injustice and exploitation of Irish people widely practised by greedy landlords and the ruling class. His Irish republicanism grew and he eventually became one of the leaders of the Easter Rising of 1916. As he was injured during the rising, when he was executed, he had to be carried on a stretcher to the prison courtyard and tied to a chair to face the firing squad. His body was initially put into a mass grave with the other republicans who were executed. He was later reburied at Arbour Hill cemetery in Dublin, along with other Easter Rising Leaders, John McBride and Patrick Pearse.

WALES

Around AD 390, pirates from Ireland started actively raiding along the Welsh coast and settling there. One of the unfortunate teenagers who was kidnapped during this period was Patricius, or young St Patrick. Born in a small village of Banwen in Wales, he was captured and sold into slavery in Ireland. During his captivity, he developed his spiritual side and, after escaping, he returned to Wales and studied to be a priest. He decided to serve God as a missionary, a calling which brought him back to Ireland. And the rest is history. This is the most widely accepted version of the story of St Patrick. Although some other accounts exist, this was the story told by Patrick himself and it is how he wanted his life to be remembered. In any case, he spent the rest of his life spreading Christianity in Ireland, creating a plethora of myths and tales along the way, and he died on 17 March in AD 460, which went on to become St Patrick's Day.

Another famous Welsh Catholic was bishop of Menevia, St David (500?-589), the patron saint of Wales. His mother was from Ireland. As well as being a great Church leader and preacher, he established St David's Cathedral and a host of churches and monastic settlements in Wales, south-west England and Brittany in France. He died on 1 March, which is called St David's Day in his honour. He was buried at St David's Cathedral.

At the beginning of the Industrial Revolution, Cardiff was still an obscure little village. However, it grew rapidly and when the railway from Cardiff to Merthyr Tydfil was built in the 1840s, approximately 50,000 Irish immigrants settled in its Grangetown and Canton districts. Irish people traditionally came to Wales to work in the coal mines and they helped develop numerous localities in the vibrant coal-mining communities in the nineteenth and twentieth centuries. In the same way, although not on as large a scale, Welsh miners went to Irish mines, such as the Allihies copper mines in County Cork which were opened in 1812. When these mines were closed, many skilled and experienced miners moved to the US to take up mining jobs there, in particular, Butte, Montana – one of the most Irish places in the US.

As was the case all across Britain, there was a huge surge of Irish immigrants to Wales during and after the Great Famine. Destitute

Irish refugees without shoes begging on the streets were a common sight and the local poorhouses were packed with them. For instance, the Pillgwenlly district of Newport had a population at that time of approximately 7,000, 1,500 of whom were Irish. Large Irish communities could also be found in Cardiff, Swansea and Merthyr Tydfil. Hibernian societies were established in Newport and then throughout Wales. These societies functioned as benefit organisations and their members were given support in the times of unemployment, illness and death.

Almost all labourers who worked at the docks and on the railways and roads in Newport in the 1840s and '50s were Irish immigrants. One of the notable features of Irish immigration in Wales was that significant numbers of them worked in the hospitality sector, such as pubs, lodging and general retail businesses.

The majority of Irish immigrants integrated well into society and became actively involved in local politics. Among them was James Murphy, who became the first Roman Catholic mayor of Newport in 1868. In the small town of Wrexham, a Catholic Irishman, John Beirne, was elected mayor in 1876. Beirne had built up a successful brewery business in the town. Former Cardiff wholesale wine and spirit merchant Patrick William Carey, from County Tipperary, likewise became mayor of Cardiff in 1894.

James Driscoll (1880-1925), also known as Peerless Jim, was a legendary boxing champion. Born in Cardiff to Irish Catholic immigrants, he grew up in Newtown, which was called Little Ireland. He became an inspiring local hero as he fought his way out of poverty by becoming the British featherweight champion.

There are two vital ports in Wales with connections to Ireland – Holyhead and Fishguard. Holyhead is the older of the two ports, dating back to the time of the Romans. These shipping routes not only carried Irish migrants to Britain but they also took mail to and fro, allowing migrants to keep in touch with their relatives and, often, send money home to pay the passage of another family member to Britain. On stepping on to Britain's shore at either Holyhead or Fishguard, Irish migrants then made their way all across Britain, settling throughout the county, though the majority headed for London. The first railway line from Holyhead to London's Euston station was opened in 1848 by the Chester and Holyhead Railway and, naturally, a large population of Irish immigrants settled in and around the Euston station area. Many people who worked at the station itself had an Irish accent and they often helped newly arrived fellow country people who did not have pre-arranged jobs or accommodation. In the twentieth century, charity workers and nuns waited at the station for troubled Irish youngsters, such as the pregnant girls and distraught teenagers who often had no idea what to do upon arriving in London. The route from Rosslare in County Wexford to Fishguard is the newer of the two routes; it was established in 1906 by the Great Western Railway. As the Fishguard harbour train arrives at London Paddington station, the area around this station also became heavily populated with Irish people. For many, the ports of Holyhead and Fishguard represented the first step on the way to a better life.

ENGLAND

There has always been a continuous flow of Irish immigration to England. Unlike going to the US or Australia, going to England was relatively easy because the transportation costs were lower and it would be easier to return to Ireland, if desired.

In many English cities, such as Liverpool, Manchester, Birmingham and London, Irish immigrants have long made up a significant proportion of the population. Irish miners could be found in Cornish mines, and hawkers, dock labourers, seasonal workers, navvies, factory workers and domestic servants were ubiquitous all across England. In the mid-nineteenth century, approximately three-quarters of all dock workers and two-thirds of miners were Irish.

The Irish migrants' prime destination during the early Victorian period was London and by 1851 there were more Irish-born people in London than in any other British city. Many had left Ireland to escape rural poverty and, as well as offering plenty of job opportunities, this large metropolitan industrial city had countless exciting things to do. Despite the often chaotic nature of the city, the lure of London proved irresistible. It was a real magnet for all immigrants, especially young people and single women.

Once in London, they tended to stick together. Although some immigrants were middle-class (generally Protestants who had had the advantage of more educational opportunities back in Ireland), most were poor Catholics and many only spoke Gaelic. It wasn't only their language or accent that made it difficult for them to mix with other people; they also suffered discrimination. Being under-privileged, impoverished and unskilled in the British framework meant that they quickly formed Irish slums or deprived Irish neighbourhoods. These areas were typically characterised by high levels of disease, vagrancy, alcoholism and squalor. One of the earliest Irish slums was located just off London's main thoroughfare, Oxford Street, within walking distance of St Patrick's church in Soho. There were also particularly heavily concentrated of Irish in Camden, Kilburn, Hammersmith, Southwark and Whitechapel.

The Great Famine was the defining moment in the history of Irish emigration. Although more people actually migrated to America than Britain during this period, Britain nevertheless received a substantial number of famine victims. Irish immigration in England kept increasing and after the Great Depression of 1929, England became the top destination for mass migration. With a huge Irish population, a disproportionate number of whom hailed from Munster, parts of London were more Irish than Ireland itself in the twentieth century. This was especially true in the 1950s, during the post-war reconstruction boom. This decade became known as the 'vanishing Irish' decade as it was the 1950s that saw more Irish immigration than any other since the famine. After the Second World War, unable to cope with the large numbers of unemployed citizens, the Irish Government deliberately let hundreds of thousands of its people leave the country as it didn't create any incentives to keep them in Ireland.

As soon as southern Ireland gained independence from Britain, the Irish found themselves dominated by the Catholic Church, which had a huge degree of power – more even than the government. During this period, there were a large number of so-called 'social casualties' who crossed the Irish Sea. In those days, getting pregnant out of wedlock was absolutely unacceptable and brought shame to the family. As a result, many pregnant girls headed to Britain to give birth or get an abortion. Other social casualties to cross the Irish Sea were criminals, prostitutes, depressed young people and traumatised people who wanted to run away not only from the Church authorities and religious institutions, but also from difficult family situations. All of these people sought, among other things, freedom and independence. Irish priests expressed their grave concerns over those people moving to 'Pagan England'. Those who left were often merely following the crowd, succumbing to peer pressure or leaving as a result of a snap decision – after an argument with a family member, for instance.

An advantage of being in London was the extensive Irish support system: plenty of Irish charity organisations, Church-organised events, County Associations, GAA groups, Irish cultural groups, Irish newspapers and dance halls could all be found in the city. The well-developed transportation system gave people a freedom of movement and an independence that made it easy to attend various social events on a regular basis. With plenty of work available if you weren't too picky, it was not difficult to fill your time. However, there were some negative aspects to life in London, such as discrimination, alcoholism, homesickness and the difficulty of finding accommodation. While women tended to find like-minded people and adapted to the change relatively easily, men who made the move often struggled to find balance.

Towards the end of the nineteenth and for much of the twentieth century, there was also a significant level of intellectual migration. On top of every social and religious force, the Censorship of Publications Act was passed by the Oireachtas, the Irish parliament, in 1929, which gave the government a stifling authoritative power over Irish cultural life. Seen as agents of social disintegration, writers couldn't read or write what they wanted. Feeling constrained and paralysed in their homeland, many of them left Ireland for London or elsewhere.

***

DISCRIMINATION

Racial discrimination against the Irish is deeply rooted in British history. In response to the continued resistance by the Irish of

British rule in Ireland, a derogatory stereotype of the Irish was planted by the English that has never completely disappeared. As a consequence, the Irish in Britain suffered from discrimination and were made to feel like outsiders for a long time. They were also the targets of hostilities for a long time, primarily because of their religion, as well as a number of political and cultural issues. Signs such as 'No Irish Need Apply' and 'No Irish or Blacks Need Apply' existed in the 1800s and were a common sight on windows and in newspaper advertisements right up until the 1950s. In Scotland, back when there were no foreign immigrants, such signs simply read 'Catholics Need Not Apply'. Many Scottish people believed that the Irish carried diseases, as evidenced by the fact that typhus was also known as 'Irish fever'.

There were plenty of poorly paid, dirty and dangerous jobs that Irish people would take in Britain, but finding accommodation was much more difficult. Navvies, in particular, suffered a great deal in the twentieth century. 'Navvy' is a shortened form of 'navigator', which formerly meant a person who does hard physical or manual labour and the vast majority of them were Irish immigrants. It is no exaggeration to say that without the Irish workforce, many British infrastructure projects would never have been built. Navvies were forced to do physically demanding jobs without medical care (they were entitled to receive it, but no one knew about it). Although it was not always the case, they typically had a bad reputation – with their muddy wellingtons and a dirty donkey coat, they frequently got involved in fights and were often drunk. Their accents were mocked and looked down on as inferior. As a result, not many people would rent rooms to them and Irish navvies had to endure sleeping in cramped and unhygienic conditions on the floor. Socially isolated and lonely, they relied on alcohol. The pub – which was coincidentally the place where they found work and got paid – was the only place where they could talk to someone.

On top of this, some unsympathetic local landlords and landladies increased rents or evicted Irish tenants for minimal reason – or sometimes for no reason at all. Some young navvies lived with sympathetic landladies who mothered them – cooking nice meals for them, washing their clothes, surprising them on their birthdays and giving them wise advice – but most of them were not so lucky. More often than not, the plight of the navvies was excruciating, despite the fact that they were the ones who were sacrificing their lives to build Britain.

Although working conditions were atrocious and quite often inhumane, there were always plenty of jobs available for Irish men if they were prepared to put up with such conditions. Some former Irish navvies even successfully established their own companies, including John Murphy from County Kerry, Pat McNicholas from County Mayo, Michael Clancy from County Clare, Pat Fitzpatrick from County Cork, Michael Joseph Gleeson and Peteen Lowery both from County Galway. Naturally these bosses tended to hire their own county men.

During the second half of the twentieth century, The Troubles in Ireland also had an impact on Irish migrants in Britain. The IRA became active again in 1969 and started a bombing campaign in Britain, especially London. Having St Patrick's Day's celebrations or showing your Irishness was unthinkable during those times. The UK police had the power to stop and search people and this was widely practised. If you were tall, happened to have red hair and an Irish accent, it was not uncommon to be stopped and held for questioning. For this reason, Irish immigrants, particularly those who crossed the Irish Sea on a regular basis, had to keep their head down in Britain. Things got gradually better after the Good Friday Agreement in 1998. St Patrick's Days festival in London resumed not long afterwards.

Although things have certainly changed for the better, old prejudices die hard and the anti-Irish feeling still somehow unconsciously runs through Britain. The difference between the Irish in Britain and the Irish in the US is that in the US things function on an ethnic basis and categorising one's ethnicity is highly important. Many people, even if their ancestors arrived centuries ago, tend to retain their racial heritage by using the word 'Irish American'. Irish Americans are well received and proud because of their ancestors' positive contribution to the country. On the other hand, in Britain the word 'Irish British' does not exist, in the same way that 'Scottish British' and 'Welsh British' are not common terms. If you are born in England to

Irish parents, you will have a British accent and will be simply called British. Scotland, Wales, England and Ireland are all part of the British Isles and each region has its own distinctive traditions and culture. So the term is political-geographical rather than ethnic.

IRISH TRAVELLERS

There are an indigenous minority people in Ireland called Travellers. While some researchers claim they are the descendants of those who were dispossessed during the Cromwellian Plantation or the Great Famine, others believe they were the original Celtic nomadic people. They are not related to Romany gypsies. The vast majority of Travellers are Roman Catholic, speak English and have Irish surnames. For centuries, they had been leaving Ireland to improve their economic status. And their migrant patterns are similar to those of settled Irish immigrants. For a start, there are more Travellers abroad than in Ireland, especially in the UK and the US, countries where they often found employment as seasonal workers and navvies. A substantial number of them emigrated during the Great Famine and after the Second World War. Although there are large settlements in rural areas in the UK, the largest populations of Travellers in England are to be found in London, Manchester, Liverpool and Birmingham. It is estimated there are approximately 15,000 in England and Wales.

MILITARY IMMIGRANTS

The Irish travelled and fought all across the globe with the British Armed Forces. In fact, the British Army has always relied on Irishmen in times of emergency since its establishment. There were no wars involving Great Britain that did not see Irish soldiers fighting for the British. The powerful expansionist British Empire probably wouldn't have seen such a success in its military exploits if it weren't for the Irishmen it counted in its ranks. The Royal Navy, which has been officially active since the sixteenth century, also consisted of a great number of Irish officers and sailors. It was thanks to the Royal Navy, which for many years was the most influential and efficient navy in the world, that the British Empire was able to explore, expand and defend their territories.

One of the notable early conflicts was the Hundred Years' War (1337–1453) against France, which saw countless Irish soldiers fight bravely for the Kingdom of England. Most of the Tudor armies were also Irish. In the 1680s, scores of Irish regiments were raised. When the union of the kingdoms of Scotland and England (including Wales) officially became the Kingdom of Great Britain in 1707, Ireland was considered as an essential part of it and six Irish Regiments were included in the British Army, despite the fact that Ireland had not been formally included in the union.

Desperately in need of soldiers, Britain somewhat relaxed the Penal Laws during the last half of the eighteenth century so that Catholics could bear arms, after which large-scale recruitment began. At the end of the eighteenth century, approximately half of the British Army soldiers were Irishmen. Needless to say, countless Irish soldiers sacrificed their lives in this way over the centuries. Some of the main reasons for joining the British Armed Forces included economic necessity, family tradition, career development, the attractive uniform, a desire for adventure, the opportunity to go abroad, and so on. Irishmen have an international reputation of being fierce and brave soldiers. That's why there is a saying that the British Empire was won by the Irish and administered by the Scottish with the profits going to the English.

As there was a long-standing tradition among the Irish of serving as mercenaries, Irish soldiers could typically be found on both sides of various conflicts and often faced each other on the battlefield. Some of the Irish soldiers who were fighting against Britain were British Army deserters who wanted to use their military skills for another cause or country. Or they could simply have found themselves out of work after one conflict, a situation which prompted them to join non-British forces as mercenaries. As an almost endless stream of enthusiastic Irish mercenaries were fighting in various European battles, Britain officially made recruitment activities in Ireland by foreign armies illegal in 1745.

Scores of Irish regiments have existed throughout British military history, even before the establishment of the British Army. Having their own regimental depots in both England and Ireland, Irish regiments were constantly forming, disbanding, amalgamating and re-forming. The Irish Guards, one of the infantry regiments of the British Army, was formed in 1900 in response to the courageous actions performed by soldiers of Irish regiments in the Second Boer War. This unit is famously called the Fighting Micks, the Micks or the Paddys.

Nearly 200 Irish soldiers have been awarded the Victoria Cross, which is the highest award available in the British military. Those who received the award had been through the Crimean War, the Indian Mutiny, two world wars and countless other British Empire campaigns. Despite the fact that Ireland was neutral during the Second World War, many Irish soldiers fought as mercenaries while ordinary immigrants in Britain were working to support the war industries.

During the First World War (1914-1918), more than 200,000 Irish people fought and nearly 50,000 of them were killed while serving in the British Army. When they left Ireland, cheering crowds saw them off but the country was transformed while they were risking their lives in the war and they came back to a staunchly nationalist Ireland where the Irish war veterans were viewed as enemies. The completely different atmosphere had been caused by the execution of Irish republicans by the British after the Easter Rising in 1916. Soldier, writer and nationalist politician Tom Kettle (1880-1916), who was later killed on the Somme in France while serving with the 16th Division, summarised those Irish soldiers' sentiments. He wrote, 'These men [the Easter Rising leaders] will go down in history as heroes and martyrs and I will go down – if I go down at all – as a bloody British officer.' Needless to say, the Irish who were involved in the war weren't just soldiers – there were also doctors, nurses, religious people and so on. Some veterans who fought in the Battle of the Somme joined the IRA upon returning in Ireland.

One of the most famous Irish migrants to serve with the British Army was James Barry (1790?-1865). Throughout history, women disguised themselves as men to survive or pursue their chosen career and James Barry was actually born Margaret Ann Bulkley, the daughter of a grocer in County Cork, who was also a niece of James Barry, an acclaimed Irish artist and professor of painting at the Royal Academy in London. After graduating with a medical degree from the University of Edinburgh, Barry moved to London and became qualified as a Regimental Assistant. As a surgeon for the British Army, he travelled all across the world, visiting places such as India, South Africa and the Caribbean. He rose to the rank of Inspector General of military hospitals. As a distinguished, pioneering doctor, he achieved the highest recovery rate of wounded and sick soldiers during the Crimean War and performed the first successful caesarean section operation in South Africa. People didn't know his real secret until he died of dysentery. He was the first female to qualify as a doctor in Britain. Embarrassed and ashamed, army officials sealed Barry's official service records for almost a hundred years.

THE IRISH LANGUAGE

As the powerful English rulers of Ireland forcefully banned the use of Irish, the number of native speakers declined dramatically in the seventeenth century and the Great Famine came as a deadly blow to the language. Patrick, also known as Pádraig, Pearse (1879-1916), an Irish nationalist and poet, famously said, '*Tír gan teanga, tír gan anam*' – a country without a language is a country without a soul. The Nobel-winning poet Seamus Heaney (1939-2013) echoed these sentiments on the importance of the language when he said:

> Not to learn Irish is to miss the opportunity of understanding what life in this country has meant and could mean in a better future. It is to cut oneself off from ways of being at home. If we regard self-understanding, mutual understanding, imaginative enhancement, cultural diversity and a tolerant political atmosphere as desirable attainments, we should remember that a knowledge of the Irish language is an essential element in their realisation.

In a way, the Irish diaspora had already come into being in Ireland because of the loss of the language, a loss which distanced them from Ireland's history and culture.

Although researchers believe some words were purely made-up or coincidental, quite a few English language phrases and everyday street slang are thought to be derived from Irish words, phrases Irish people often used or even Irish-related phrases adapted by non-Irish people. As a substantial number of Irish native speakers arrived in the wake of the famine hitting the *Gaeltacht* (regions where native Irish speakers live), there can be no doubt that they mixed words and phrases from their own language into English when they started using it on a daily basis. A plethora of Irish words and Irish-related phrases thus became part of the English language.

For example, the word 'hooligan' originated from Patrick Hooligan (it may have been that his name was actually Houlihan) from County Limerick who was an Irish bouncer and gangster in London. According to various newspaper articles of the late nineteenth century, the Hooligan Boys in Lambeth, South London, which was a predominantly Irish area, were actively involved in all sorts of misdemeanours.

'Tory' was originally used to refer to an Irish outlaw. The term is derived from the word '*tóir*', which means 'to pursue'. It first became the word used to describe English Jacobite supporters and later English Conservatives.

'Boycott' means 'to ostracise' and comes from Captain Charles Boycott, an English land agent who was ostracised by tenant farmers in County Mayo in 1872. Not only did he refused to reduce rents; he also began evicting those who couldn't pay. Angry tenants stopped working for him and in the end they succeeded in kicking him out of Ireland.

'Lynch' means 'to punish or kill without a legal trial'. The term could have originated in Ireland when Mayor Lynch of Galway hanged his son from a window in his castle for murdering a Spanish seafarer as he couldn't find an executioner. However, the following American story might be more plausible. Irish American Charles Lynch (1736-1796) was a Virginia Justice of the Peace who presided over extralegal trials during the American Revolutionary War. 'Lynch's Law' came to mean unauthorised punishment.

'*Bog*' is a Gaelic word meaning 'soft' or 'an area of wet muddy ground'. '*Bard*' is used to describe a poet or someone who recites epics and lyrical verse, often associated with the oral tradition. 'Brogue' implies an Irish accent and is derived from '*bróg*', or an untanned shoe worn by Irish and Scottish people. 'Whiskey' is a straightforward anglicised term, which comes from '*uisce beatha*', meaning 'the water of life'. Irish monks started using it in the Middle Ages. 'Galore' comes from '*go leor*', which means 'enough' or 'plenty' and 'glen' stems from '*gleann*', which means a narrow valley.

Other words that reputedly have Irish links include: babe, bailiff, beak, boot, boss, buddy, bunk, cop, cant, darn, dig, donnybrook, dude, geek, gibberish, giggle, gob, graft, hunch, ice, jazz, jerks, joint, kitty, knack, mug, poker, scam, shanty, trousers, swells, shank, shanty, smacker, spunk, pet, propaganda, queer, quid, quirky, rookie, slogan, stiff, slat, slum, slugger, slug, smack, smashing, twig and whale, to list but a few. Commonly used phrases derived from Irish or related to the Irish include 'Paddy wagon', 'the fighting Irish', 'taking the Mick', 'Bob's your uncle', 'duke it out' and 'double cross'.

As well as influencing the English language, Irish migrants had an impact on many other aspects of British culture.

PHILANTHROPISTS

Irish philanthropists had a significant influence in Britain by founding some of the leading charities. The great-grandson of the man who set up the Guinness Brewery was Edward Guinness, 1st Earl of Iveagh (1847-1927) and he founded the Guinness Trust in 1890. His charitable housing association has built more than 60,000 homes for homeless people all across England.

The founder of the Barnardo's home, Dubliner Thomas John Barnardo (1845-1905), was a medical doctor who converted to Protestantism at the age of 16. He witnessed the chaotic effects of the Industrial Revolution in London and saw that an unprecedented number of children were on the street after being maimed in factories – and life didn't get much easier for people when they grew up. The population growth exacerbated poverty levels and was a contributing factor in the spread of disease. On top of all that, unemployment was rife. Barnardo initially set up a school for underprivileged children in London's East End and many homes for children were established shortly afterwards. Girls were taught domestic skills and the boys acquired a craft or trade. Barnardo also helped the babies of unmarried mothers and he is rightly considered a pioneer of children's charity.

INVENTORS

Some life-changing inventions were the work of Irish immigrants. Robert Boyle (1627-1691) was born in Lismore Castle, County Waterford. His father was 1st Earl of Cork. Boyle was a chemist, physicist and philosopher. He was educated at Eton College and University College, Oxford, before finally settling in London. In order to facilitate scientific discussion and experiments, he co-founded the Royal Society of London, of which he became president. He is largely responsible for establishing the foundations of modern chemistry.

Major Walter Gordon Wilson (1874-1957) from Blackrock, County Dublin, studied at Cambridge and became a trained mechanical engineer. Sponsored by the First Lord of the Admiralty, Winston Churchill long before he became British prime minister, Wilson, who was a member of the British Royal Naval Air Service along with British engineer William Tritton, invented the modern tank in 1915, which revolutionised modern warfare.

The father of the tractor is Harry Ferguson (1884-1960) from County Down. He was a bicycle repairman and engineer who created the modern version of the agricultural tractor. A son of a farmer, he also invented the first four-wheel-drive Formula One car, as well as building and flying his own aeroplane, making him the first person to do so on the British Isles.

EXPLORERS

Ireland has produced some remarkable explorers. A naval officer and adventurer, Sir Robert McClure (1807-1873) was born in County Wexford, educated at Eton and the Royal Military Academy Sandhurst, after which he joined the Royal Navy. As commander of HMS *Investigator*, he discovered the Northwest Passage, which links the Pacific and Atlantic oceans through Arctic North America. He achieved this by completing the journey by ship and overland during an expedition across Banks Island, one of the Canadian Arctic Archipelagos. His journals were later published as *The Discovery of the North-West Passage by HMS Investigator*.

Some of the most inspiring figures during the heroic age of Polar exploration were Sir Ernest Shackleton (1874-1922) and Tom Crean (1877-1938). Shackleton was born into an Anglo-Irish family in County Kildare and moved to London as a child with his father, who was a doctor. After joining the merchant navy, he undertook various expeditions and is best known for leading three British expeditions to the Antarctic. Although he may not be recognised internationally, Kerryman Crean's contribution was as valuable as Shackleton's. After running away from home at the age of 15, he joined the Royal Navy. He started off as an ordinary seaman but with his distinguished ability and skills, he was gradually promoted to higher-ranking positions. In fact, he was the most prominent member of three of the four major British expeditions to the Antarctic. Known as a tough explorer and a cheerful companion, he was promoted to first-class officer and earned three Polar medals. A glacier and a peak were named in his honour.

IRISH BISHOPS

Just as Irish priests dominated the Catholic Church in England, most of the Archbishops of Westminster were Irish or of Irish descent. The first Archbishop of Westminster after the re-establishment of the Catholic hierarchy was Nicholas Wiseman (1802-1865). Born in Seville, Spain, to Irish parents from County Waterford, he became archbishop in 1850 and was immediately elevated to cardinal. He held this position until he passed away in office.

Francis Alphonsus Bourne (1861-1935) was born in Clapham, London, to an Irish mother. He went on to serve as bishop of Southwark, where the population is predominantly Irish. After being appointed in 1903, he became cardinal in 1911 and remained in office until he died.

The first papal representative to deal with the Catholic hierarchy in Africa was Arthur Hinsley (1865-1943). He was born in North Yorkshire to Irish parents. He retired after becoming ill, but was called out of retirement to become archbishop. He served from 1935 to 1937.

Bernard William Griffin (1899-1956) was born in Birmingham, but was of Irish descent. He started his service as archbishop in 1943, became cardinal in 1946 and died in office. As he was the archbishop when Irish immigration to England reached its peak, he was the most hands-on archbishop in history. He was constantly attending Irish events, both religious and social, such as GAA and County Associations. His name was repeatedly mentioned in Irish and Catholic newspaper articles. To cater and provide for the growing Irish population, he was actively involved in recruiting locally grown Irish priests and building religious schools, institutions and organisations. He also helped establish the Camden Irish Centre and donated money to various Irish clubs and groups.

John Carmel Heenan (1905-1975) was born in Ilford, just outside of London, to Irish parents. During the Second World War, he broadcasted on the BBC Empire Service to an American audience as part of a series called 'Britain Speaks'. With his articulate and persuasive tone, he became famous for his public speaking as well as his newspaper articles. He was appointed archbishop in 1963 and he served until his death. He was raised to cardinal in 1965.

SPORT

Irish immigrants brought their sports with them and have been playing Gaelic football and hurling in Britain for centuries. The London

Gaelic Athletic Association (GAA) was officially established in 1896 to better organise the various clubs that had been formed.

The most instrumental person was Liam McCarthy (1853-1928). Born in Southwark, London, to Irish parents from County Cork, he grew up in a pure Irish environment – speaking Gaelic and playing hurling. He gained a sense of Irishness that was much stronger than that of his parents. In his time, GAA players were politically active and quite often members of the Irish Republican Brotherhood. McCarthy is best known for creating the Liam McCarthy Cup, which is offered to the winners of the All-Ireland Senior Hurling Championship.

McCarthy's friend in the GAA, Sam Maguire (1879-1927), came from County Cork. After moving to London, he became a major football player and a prominent figure on the London GAA field. He famously recruited Irish revolutionary leader Michael Collins (1890-1922) to play with him while Collins was working in the post office in West Kensington and living in Hammersmith. The Sam Maguire Cup is his namesake and is given to the winners of the All-Ireland Senior Football Championship each year.

As a team needs a strong leader with good organisational skills in order to stand the test of time, dozens of GAA teams were hastily set up (often in a pub) only to disappear shortly thereafter. Official matches were suspended during the Second World War, but the GAA in London became active again after the Allied victory and serious matches were regularly played at the Mitcham Stadium in South London and, in the 1950s, Wembley Stadium in North London. Whenever there was a match, all tickets were instantly sold out and the stadium was always packed with excited Irish immigrants. Irish VIPs, such as politicians and bishops, were often invited to such matches.

Outside of the GAA, the oldest Irish sports team in England is Liverpool St Helens Rugby Football Club, which was established in 1857. Another notable rugby team is Dewsbury Celtic, based in West Yorkshire. Famine immigrants who were working as mill workers and general labourers in the area started Dewsbury Shamrocks in 1879 and later renamed it Dewsbury Celtic. Irish immigrants also formed the London Irish Rugby Football Club, also known as the Exiles, in 1898.

Irish immigrants in Edinburgh established the Hibernian Football Club in 1875. A Sligo missionary, Brother Walfrid, formed the Celtic Football Club in Glasgow in 1887. The name 'Celtic' is pronounced 'Seltik' and the club was initially started to raise funds for poor children in Glasgow. Dundee United Football Club was created in 1909 after the demise of Dundee Harp, which had been established in 1879 and then renamed Dundee Hibernian.

Without Irish footballers or footballers of Irish descent, there would be no English football teams at all. They were not only players but also hugely involved at management level. Notable early clubs they also helped to found include Sheffield Football Club (established in 1857), Notts County Football Club (1862), Stoke City Football Club (1863), Nottingham Forest Football Club (1865), Aston Villa Football Club (1874), Manchester United (1878), Everton (1878), Manchester City Football Club (1880 – originally established as St Mark's), Tottenham Hotspur Football Club (1882), Queens Park Rangers Football Club (1886 – as a result of an amalgamation of Christchurch Rangers and St Jude's), Arsenal (1886), Liverpool Football Club (1892), Chelsea Football Club (1905) and Leeds United (1919). English football clubs garner huge support and devoted fan bases among the Irish in both Ireland and Britain.

ARTISTS

In order to gain a wider audience, have their work recognised, be stimulated by other artists and, most importantly, make a living, artists and writers often move to bigger cities. Irish people typically left Ireland for London or other British cities, not only because of the large populations and markets but also in search of intellectual and artistic freedom. There is no shortage of Irish artists and entertainers in Britain. One of the most famous rock bands of the twentieth century, the Beatles, had two members of Irish descent: Paul McCartney and John Lennon. George Harrison and Ringo Starr are also said to have some Irish blood somewhere. So did George Melly and members of the Searchers, the Animals, the Smiths … the list is endless. As well as that, many Irish musicians, such as Rory Gallagher, Van Morrison, the

Nolans, Phil Lynott's Skid Row and Thin Lizzy came to England to build a bigger fan base and, in doing so, they paved the way for future performers from Ireland. Spike Milligan was one of the most beloved comedians in Britain. Cecile Day-Lewis came to England and became an accomplished and well-known poet and his son, Daniel Day-Lewis, went on to become an internationally acclaimed actor.

The Bristol School of Artists, an informal group of landscape artists working in Bristol, England, was set up in the early nineteenth century. The Bristol School became the most inspiring place for landscape painters and many of them went on to have exhibitions in London, where there are some world-class art museums. One of these landscape painters was James Arthur O'Connor (1792-1841), a distinguished artist who was originally from Ireland. After coming to England, he began exhibiting at the Royal Academy.

Born in Ennis, County Clare, William Mulready (1786-1863) moved to London with his family. He studied at the Royal Academy and went on to become a famous landscape and genre painter in London. He is also known for his academic studies and his illustrations for books. He designed the first penny postage envelope in Britain.

Francis Danby (1793-1861) was a romantic painter and became widely known as the father of the present school of Bristolian landscape painting. He came to London with his artist friends James Arthur O'Connor and George Petrie (1790-1866), who was also an accomplished painter, writer and archaeologist. Danby's work was very well received on the London art scene and his influence on other budding artists was considerable.

Cork man Daniel Maclise (1806-1870) built a reputation as a great portrait painter who spent most of his adult life in London. Apart from his famous portraits and historic paintings, he also illustrated various books, including some by Charles Dickens.

Sir John Lavery (1856-1941), from Belfast, and his wife Lady Hazel were British statesman Winston Churchill's first mentors. A gifted all-rounder, Churchill went on to become a proficient painter, producing 500 paintings over his lifetime.

As the Irish are known for their way with words, many amateur and professional Irish writers and journalists can be found in British media and publishing industry. Dubliner William Howard Russell (1820-1907) was one of the most distinguished reporters in Britain. He wrote articles and stories for various newspapers, including *The Times*, and was best known for his coverage of wars, notably the Crimean War.

Another regular fixture on Fleet Street, Thomas Power O'Connor (1848-1929), or T.P. O'Connor, was born in Athlone, County Westmeath. After moving to London, he worked as a journalist for the *Daily Telegraph* and famously covered the Franco-Prussian War. He later became a Member of Parliament in the House of Commons. He also founded various newspapers and journals, including *The Sun*.

Alfred Charles William Harmsworth (1865-1922) from Dublin was one of the most accomplished newspaper publishers in the history of the British press. He was a pioneer in the field of tabloid journalism. Coming from a rather impoverished background, he was exceptionally ambitious and driven. He bought the poverty-stricken *London Evening News*, saved it from bankruptcy and transformed it. In 1896, he started the *Daily Mail* and it was an instant hit. Some of the reasons why 'the penny newspaper for one halfpenny' became so popular was that he made all news stories much shorter and accessible, and included fun stories such as political and social gossip, as well as women's interest articles. Among other newspapers he established was the *Daily Mirror*. He also saved a couple of impoverished newspapers, including the *Observer*, and secured control of *The Times*. He was made Baron Northcliffe for his accomplishments.

Dubliner Dion Boucicault was born Dionysius Lardner Boursiquot (1820-1890) and became one of the most distinguished playwrights and actors during the Victorian period in Britain as well as in the US.

The Brontë sisters, Charlotte (1816-1855), Emily (1818-1848) and Ann (1820-1849), were born in Yorkshire to the Revd Patrick Brontë (originally 'Brunty') from County Down. The sisters first published a collection of their poems under the pseudonyms of Currer, Ellis and Acton Bell as there was considerable prejudice against female writers at the time. Charlotte's *Jane Eyre*, Emily's *Wuthering Heights* and Anne's *The Tenant of Wildfell Hall* are nowadays considered masterpieces of British literature.

Living in London opened up a whole new world to many people. Although Abraham 'Bram' Stoker (1847-1912) was more of a passive recipient of life, his intellectual curiosity was stimulated by just being in the leading global city. Born in Dublin into a Protestant family, he began his writing career after studying at Trinity College. He moved to London with his wife to work in the Lyceum theatre with Henry Irving, a popular actor in those days. This was a mind-altering experience that opened many doors for Stoker. He made various acquaintances and got to know high-profile people in the literary world. He wrote a horror novel, *Dracula*, and other books after getting inspiration from the different people he met and the various places he visited during his travels.

George Augustus Moore (1852-1933) was born in Carra, Country Mayo. He first moved to Paris to study art as he initially wanted to be a painter rather than a writer. After giving up on his dreams of becoming an artist, he moved to London and started writing. Although he occasionally ignited controversy, the prolific writer published some distinguished poems and novels during his lifetime.

One writer who is generally considered British rather than Irish is Oscar Wilde (1854-1900). Born in Dublin to wealthy Anglo-Irish intellectual parents, he went to England to study at Oxford. As he did not come back to Ireland and did not write in or about Ireland, he was not affected by censorship and other Irish restrictions. The gifted writer, witty conversationalist and master of the English language thrived in the British literary scene; it is said that the first thing he forgot at Oxford was his Irish accent. One of the few observations he made about the Irish summarises the relationship between the English and the Irish – 'If one could only teach the English how to talk and the Irish how to listen, society would be quite civilised.'

George Bernard Shaw (1856-1950) also permanently moved to Britain and spent the rest of his life in a country house in Hertfordshire, England. He was awarded the Nobel Prize in Literature in 1925 and an Oscar in 1938. As well as being a prolific playwright and writer, he was one of the founders of the London School of Economics. His sentiment towards Ireland is summed up by his remark, 'I showed my appreciation of my native land in the usual Irish way by getting out of it as soon as I possibly could.' When the Irish Club in Eaton Square was opened, a place where Irish movers and shakers used to hang out, Shaw received an invitation from the club but rejected with the reply:

> Irish people in England should join English clubs and avoid each other like the plague. If they flock together like geese, they might as well have never left Ireland. They don't admire, nor even like one another. In English clubs they are always welcome. More fools the English perhaps; but the two are so foreign that they have much to learn from their association and co-operation.

Sir Arthur Conan Doyle (1859-1930) never lived in Ireland but was born in Edinburgh to Catholic Irish parents. A physician by profession, he moved to London to work as an ophthalmologist and started writing seriously at around the same time. The meticulous scientist wrote his famous Sherlock Holmes books in London.

The recipient of the 1923 Nobel Prize in Literature, William Butler Yeats (1865-1939) called Dublin 'the blind and ignorant town', but he didn't completely leave Ireland. In fact, he was constantly on the move and kept a foot in both ponds. He was born and raised in Ireland but studied and spent a substantial amount of time in London. While in London, he organised a literature group in Chiswick in the west of London and played an influential part in both British and Irish literary circles. He also wrote considerably about Irish nationalism. He was offered the British knighthood in 1915 but rejected it while keeping his British pension until his death. The often-cited quotation penned by him – 'Being Irish, he had an abiding sense of tragedy, which sustained him through temporary periods of joy' – resonates with millions of Irish immigrants.

One of the earliest writers and playwrights who wrote about working-class people in Ireland was Seán O'Casey (1880-1964). He moved to England permanently because he felt bitter that the Abbey Theatre, the national theatre in his native country, rejected his play, *The Silver Tassie*, which was about the imperialist First World War and the suffering of the people.

Although Patrick Kavanagh (1904-1967) didn't stay in London long, when he left for London, he acknowledged that 'Ireland was a fine place to daydream in, but London was a great materialist city where my dreams might crystallise into something more enduring than a winning smile on the face of an Irish colleen – or landscape'. He knew deep down that, from a purely practical point of view, Irish writers leave because sentimental praise is 'no use in the mouth of a hungry man'.

Samuel Beckett (1906-1989), who spent most of his life in Paris and often visited London, also had a bad experience with Ireland, which he referred to as 'an intellectually barren cultural wasteland'. When he left, he never intended to come back to his homeland. The Athlone writer John Broderick (1924-1989), who moved to England, summed up the feelings of many: 'Ireland is a great country to die in, but not a place to live in.'

2

USA

We all thought Christopher Columbus was the first European who found the New World, didn't we? But it was actually a humble monk called St Brendan, from County Kerry, who made that voyage – almost 1,000 years before the Italian explorer.

America has always been a sanctuary for the Irish and has taken in a considerable number of Irish migrants over the years. They were both forced and voluntary immigrants who arrived individually or en masse. The patterns of settlement and integration varied depending on the different waves of migrants at different times. According to the US Census Bureau, there were about 34 million US residents who claimed Irish ancestry in 2012. Plus, it is estimated that up to 7 million Scots-Irish are there. Many of these people have never even set foot in Ireland.

By 1820, when the US Government's detailed immigration statistics became available, Irish people already constituted the greatest single immigrant group. In the 1820s, 43 per cent of immigrants were from Ireland, but Irish migration to America soared during the Great Famine in the 1850s – the greatest human tragedy of the nineteenth century – when large numbers of Irish people crossed the Atlantic Ocean on the infamous coffin ships. A sea of people, mainly Catholic but not all poverty-stricken, got on such ships but conditions on board were so atrocious that between 20 and 50 per cent wouldn't make it to America. When someone died on board, their body was thrown into the ocean. For this reason, sharks followed the ships. Even making it ashore was not a guarantee of survival as a large number of the new arrivals were too weak to stand on their own feet and died shortly after arriving. Anyone who survived the coffin ships were the ultimate survivors.

Emigration to the US continued until around the Great Depression in 1929, despite the creation of the Irish Free State in 1921.

The large presence of Irish people on American shores added a distinctive flavour to the so-called melting pot. Irish immigrants had an enormous influence on the way American society was governed as they set about raising families, building communities and making a place for themselves in their adoptive country. With innumerable inspirational rags-to-riches stories, there are certainly good vibes surrounding the Irish in the US. They were politicians, soldiers, trade union activists, Hollywood actors, baseball players and boxing champions. They were the ones who achieved the American dream and became role models for all Americans.

THE SCOTS-IRISH

Early Irish immigrants who came to the US collectively in the seventeenth century were Protestants, mainly Presbyterians, from Ulster. An almost endless stream of Scots-Irish (called the Scotch-Irish in the US) arrived every year and formed their own communities, notably in Pennsylvania, Virginia and the Appalachian and Allegheny Mountain region.

The cost of the passage to the US during this time was expensive, approximately half the yearly wages of a labourer. However, one way to come to the US was as an indentured servant. This was where the captain of the ship would pay the passage money and, on arrival in the US, he would then sell the person's labour to a prospective employer. The immigrant would then work as an indentured servant to pay off his passage fees for a specified period of time – up to seven years. This method of migration proved very popular with the Scots-Irish and nine out of ten indentured servants in colonial regions of

America were Scots-Irish or Catholic Irish in the early eighteenth century. However, burdened with long-term labour contracts, quite a few of them escaped from their masters. The majority of early indentured servants settled in Pennsylvania, New Hampshire, Maine and Massachusetts.

These early migrants were principally responsible for establishing blue-collar America, various pioneer institutions, the military services, the Bible Belt, and so on. They became politicians and business owners, and helped shape American culture, especially when it came to country, western and folk music.

The Scots-Irish Presbyterians contributed greatly to the establishment of several academic institutions. One of the most distinguished is the College of New Jersey, which was established in 1746 to train New Light Presbyterian ministers and was the forerunner of Princeton University.

In the nineteenth century, more than 200,000 Scots-Irish settled in the thirteen American colonies. Some of the main reasons for this mass exodus from Ulster were a series of droughts and rising rents imposed by absentee landlords. Due to the large number of people from Ulster who settled in Pennsylvania, the region became the main stronghold of Scots-Irish immigrants.

Thomas Mellon (1813-1908) was one of the most notable Scots-Irish immigrants. Born in County Tyrone, he came to the US with his family and settled in Westmoreland County, Pennsylvania. Versatile Thomas was a lawyer, judge and banker. Together with his sons, he founded Mellon Bank in Pittsburgh. The vigorous Mellon dynasty further founded and controlled Gulf Oil (Chevron-Texaco), Westinghouse (CBS Corporation and Siemens), Alcoa, Rockwell, *The Pittsburgh Tribune-Review*, New York Shipbuilding, Carborundum Corporation and Koppers, to name but a few.

Another eminent settler was James H. Laughlin (1806-1882), who was born in County Down. After becoming a junior partner in the iron business of Benjamin Franklin Jones in Pittsburgh in 1854, he became a pioneer of the iron and steel industry and the company changed its name to Jones and Laughlin in 1861. Laughlin also gave back to the community by contributing large sums to educational institutions. As well as being the first president of the Western Theological Seminary in Pittsburgh, he also founded the Pennsylvania Female College, the forerunner of Chatham University.

From their humble beginnings, a horde of Irish immigrants showed a shrewd political sense and some of them even served as presidents. After Scots-Irish Andrew Jackson became the seventh president (1829-1837), a considerable number of prominent Scots-Irish/Irish Catholic immigrants and descendants followed in his footsteps. Although many American presidents can trace their ancestry back to Ireland somehow, some of the more notable ones include: James Knox Polk (eleventh president, 1845-49), James Buchanan (fifteenth president, 1857-61), Andrew Johnson (seventeenth president, 1865-69), Ulysses S. Grant (eighteenth president, 1869-77), Chester A. Arthur (twenty-first president, 1881-85), Grover Cleveland (twenty-second and twenty-fourth president, 1885-89), Benjamin Harrison (twenty-third president, 1889-93), William McKinley (twenty-fifth president, 1897-1901), Theodore Roosevelt (twenty-sixth president, 1901-09), William Howard Taft (twenty-seventh president, 1909-13), Woodrow Wilson (twenty-eighth president, 1913-21), Warren G. Harding (twenty-ninth president, 1921-23), Harry S. Truman (thirty-third president, 1945-53), John F. Kennedy (thirty-fifth president, 1961-63), Richard Nixon (thirty-seventh president, 1969-74), Jimmy Carter (thirty-ninth president, 1977-81), Ronald Reagan (fortieth president, 1981-89), George H.W. Bush (forty-first president, 1989-93), Bill Clinton (forty-second president, 1993-2001) and Barack Obama (forty-fourth president, 2009-).

The term 'Jacksonian Democracy' was coined by Andrew Jackson (1767-1845) and his supporters. Jacksonianism is basically a political movement that represented a diverse national coalition and became the dominant political code of America's working class. Compared with his predecessors and colleagues, Jackson was unique and unassuming. Born in a log cabin, he was mocked by his opposition parties and called a jackass. To embarrass him, some publications printed a cartoon of him and a character sketch – a centaur figure, which was half Jackson and half donkey. Instead of taking offence, he took advantage of it by using it as his logo. It went on to become the emblem of the US Democratic Party. As the first US president who did not come from an aristocratic, intellectual, elite background, he was a breath of fresh air and he succeeded in changing the American political structure.

NAVVIES

It is no exaggeration to say that without Irish construction workers, American infrastructure would never have been built at all. They played a key role in the Industrial Revolution during the nineteenth century, working on everything from high-profile building projects, such as the Erie Canal, the Union Pacific railroad and the Empire State building, to countless uncelebrated bridges and roads. The mining industry was also largely developed by Irish immigrants' toil and sweat. Of course, such work was not without human sacrifices – the job itself was extremely dangerous and many died in on-site accidents. Also, countless Irish workers died of illnesses and diseases such as cholera, malaria and yellow fever due to their unhygienic lifestyle and horrendous working conditions.

The Irish played a major role in the construction of the Erie Canal. Work started on the canal in 1817 and it was completed in 1825. The canal was the first transportation system to link the coastal ports in New York and Great Lakes. It changed the methods of transportation dramatically in terms of cost and time as there were no steamships or railways at the time. However, working conditions were far from good. Not only was the terrain mountainous and the work – digging through limestone – difficult, there was also the risk of contracting malaria, which killed more than a thousand workers. With a total workforce of about 50,000 people, a substantial number of both Catholic Irish and Scots-Irish immigrants were working on-site. Many of them had just arrived from Ireland. It is estimated that approximately 5,000 Scots-Irish were recruited in Northern Ireland to work on the canal. They were paid between 35 and 80 cents a day for ten to twelve hours of physically demanding work. As they progressed westward, Irish immigrants started forming communities along the canal.

The New Basin Canal in New Orleans, Louisiana, also couldn't have been built without a workforce of Irish immigrants. They were paid one dollar a day when construction started in 1832. Again, they were killed in great numbers – more than 8,000 died, either while working or from yellow fever, cholera or malaria. When they died, they were simply and quickly buried in the levee and roadway fill beside the canal. There is a song which commemorates those who lost their lives prematurely:

Ten thousand Micks, they swung their picks
To dig the New Canal
But the cholera was stronger 'n' they
An twice it killed them awl.

This highly risky work in mosquito-infested areas was done mainly by Irish immigrants as they were considered less valuable than slave labour in the Deep South. If an Irishman died, it was easy to replace him at no cost as Irish immigrants continued to arrive in the US en masse but slaves were considered valuable assets and a dead slave typically resulted in the loss of around 1,000 dollars in those times. To cater for a growing number of Irish parishioners, St Patrick's church was founded in 1833 in the city centre of New Orleans.

The Union Pacific Railroad was also built primarily by Irish labourers. The Union Pacific line was constructed westward from Council Bluffs, Iowa, to meet the Central Pacific line, which was built eastward from Sacramento, California, and the two lines were connected at Promontory Summit, Utah in 1869. This was the first transcontinental railroad in America and its construction resulted in countless casualties. Irish workers were paid between 2 and 4 dollars per day and assigned to do the most dangerous tasks with the highest accident rates. Due to the large numbers of immigrants killed at work, there was a saying that stated that there was an Irishman buried under every railroad tie – and it was no exaggeration.

Construction of the Empire State Building began on St Patrick's Day, 17 March 1930, as the president of Empire State, Inc., Al Smith, was partly of Irish Catholic descent. More than 3,000 workers were recruited for the construction work, a substantial number of them Irish immigrants.

The Brooklyn Bridge, connecting Manhattan and Brooklyn over the East River in New York, was completed in 1883. It was also the Irish immigrants who came in droves to work on the construction of the longest suspension bridge in the world at the time. Up to thirty people were killed – some fell to their death, some were killed by falling equipment, while others were killed during the cable rigging – and many of them bore Irish surnames.

BRIDGETS

As well as the Irish construction and mine workers, countless Irish girls and women worked as domestic servants in middle-class American homes. Affectionately called Bridgets, English-speaking Irish women could be found throughout American cities in the late nineteenth and early twentieth centuries. They assimilated relatively easily into the local society as most of them started working as domestic servants during their teenage years, so it was easy for them to adapt to middle-class ways and values.

Irish domestic workers in the US were treated much better than their counterparts in Ireland and the UK. Although they lived in tiny attics or cellars and worked long hours, the majority of girls seemed to enjoy their newfound independence, both financial and psychological, and many managed to stay positive and gregarious by going to social functions with friends and attending church services when not working.

SOLDIERS

No wars or battles in the US occurred without the presence of Irish soldiers. There have been literally millions of significant Irish and Irish American officers and soldiers over the course of military history in the US. To acknowledge their incalculable contribution, Irish troops often lead St Patrick's Day's parades in the US. For those stationed in foreign countries, a St Patrick's Day Run is also a way of marking the long tradition of Irish people or people of Irish descent serving in the US military.

During the American Revolutionary War (1775-1783), also known as the US War of Independence, hundreds of thousands of Irish officers and soldiers fought on both sides. This political upheaval started between the residents of the thirteen colonies of British America and the colonial government, which represented the British Crown. As immeasurable numbers of Irish and Irish Americans, both Scots-Irish and Catholic Irish volunteers, were part of the revolution, Lord Mountjoy once complained to the British Parliament that 'We have lost America through the Irish'. Irish immigrants and Irish Americans also signed the Declaration of Independence and the Constitution. Andrew Jackson, the first Scots-Irish president, actually fought in the American Revolution and was held as a prisoner of war.

One of the most influential Irish officers during the American Revolutionary War was Richard Montgomery (1738-1775), who served as major general in the Continental Army. Born in Swords, County Dublin, he studied at Trinity College and initially joined the British Army. He eventually emigrated to the US and settled in New York. When the war broke out, he was offered a position as brigadier general in the Continental Army. As a capable military man, he gradually climbed up the ranks.

Another remarkable Irishman was John Barry (1745-1803) from Tacumshane, County Wexford. He was the first captain to command a US warship under the Continental flag during the war. The son of a poor Irish farmer, he eventually rose from the modest position of cabin boy to commander of the entire US feet. After earning the title of commodore, he was called the Father of the American Navy.

Later, a considerable number of famine immigrants joined the US Army as they were promised land and citizenship after they had served, but the reality was that many of them suffered from atrocious discrimination and prejudice under Protestant officers and eventually deserted their regiments. Some of them joined foreign armies to fight against the US.

The American Civil War (1861-1865) was one of the most deci-
sive and bloody conflicts in US history. It was fought between the
Confederate States of America and the Union, led by Abraham
Lincoln. The two sides were fighting over slavery, states' rights
and other issues. Scared of losing their jobs to freed African slaves,
approximately 25,000 Irish fought on the confederate side but the
vast majority of the Irish – approximately 150,000 – joined the
Union Army. In the end, the Confederates lost and slavery was abolished. The Union side achieved victory because it had more soldiers
and guns. It is no exaggeration to say that the Irish soldiers played
a big part of their win. But the truth is that most Irish immigrants
had settled in anti-slavery states, so they had no choice but to join
the war. They accepted their fate by forming their own regiments,
such as the 69th New York State Volunteers, with their own priests
by their side.

Irish and Irish American officers served with distinction on both
sides. One of the high-profile officers of the Union side was General
Michael Corcoran (1827-1863). Born in Ballymote, County Sligo,
he was descended from Patrick Sarsfield of the Jacobite Wars on his
mother's side. He was one of the founders of the Fenian Brotherhood
in the US before he joined the Union Army.

A Waterford man, Thomas Francis Meagher (1823-1867) was
the leader of the Young Irelanders in the Rebellion of 1848. He
was captured and sent to a penal colony in Tasmania, Australia but
escaped and fled to the US. After joining the Union Army, he rose
to the rank of brigadier general. He was responsible for recruiting Irish soldiers and was in charge of the Irish Brigade. Born in
Leighlinbridge, County Carlow, Myles Walter Keogh (1840-1876)
also worked his way up and became lieutenant colonel by the end
of the war. He was known as a great military man with strong
leadership ability.

In the same way, scores of Irish officers fought for the
Confederate states. Dubliner William Montague Browne (1827-
1883) was a general who had been serving in the British Army.
A native of Ovens, County Cork, Patrick Cleburne (1828-1864)
served as major general. Originally from Galway, Richard William
Dowling (1838-1867) was lieutenant commander and his unit,

the Jefferson Davis Guard, was awarded a medal for their remarkable war effort. General Joseph Finnegan (1814-1885) was born in Clones, County Monaghan, and emigrated to Florida, where he worked as a lawyer, farmer and railroad builder. Versatile and skilful, Finnegan was firmly established in the US even before joining the war. Tyrone man James Hagan (1822-1901) served as colonel and commanded the brigade. Before joining the army, he was a planter and businessman in Philadelphia. Cork man Walter P. Lane (1817-1892) initially went to Texas to join the Mexican War of Independence and finally became a Confederate general back in the US. Patrick Theodore Moore (1821-1883), from County Galway, also served as a general.

The sheer number of Irish troops meant that a great many were killed and injured. The people who tended wounded and sick soldiers on the battlefield were primarily Irish nuns from numerous communities, such as the Sisters of Mercy, who travelled to remote areas with the regiments. It is estimated that at least 600 nuns from twelve religious communities served as army nurses in the US. Irish nuns also played an important role in the development of most early hospitals throughout the US.

During the American Civil War, over 400 women fought pretending to be men. Some of them had no choice as they needed to make a living, while others fought along with their husbands and brothers in order to be with them. The most outstanding of these was Jennie Hodgers (1843-1915) from Clogherhead, County Louth. When she was young, her father dressed her up like a boy so she could get a job as the impoverished family struggled to make ends meet. Her mother died when she was still a child and she later emigrated to the US. The pint-sized Hodgers enlisted in the 95th Illinois Infantry as Albert Cashier and took part in more than forty battles as a brave and accomplished infantryman. After the war, she came back to Saunemin, Illinois, and worked in many different jobs, including as a cemetery worker, church janitor, street lamplighter, shepherd and chauffeur – all made possible because of her status as a man. During the time when women didn't have the right to vote, Hodgers could vote and was able to collect a veteran's pension. When she was admitted to the hospital due to dementia, the secret was finally discovered. Her mental state further deteriorated as she was forced to wear women's clothing. Not accustomed to walking in strange clothing, she tripped and broke her hip, which left her bedridden for the rest of her life.

One of the crucial technologies many countries sought to develop during wartime was the submarine. Engineers had been attempting to build one since the eighteenth century but developing the submarine was a rather tricky business. Through trial and error, it was engineer John Philip Holland (1840-1914) who eventually developed the first submarine for the US Navy. Born in Liscannor, County Clare, he emigrated to the US, where he taught and worked for an engineering firm, and started designing submarines. A member of the Irish Republican Brotherhood, Holland tried to contribute to the cause of Ireland. He built a small submarine, the Fenian Ram, in 1879 for the Irish Fenian Society. After many different experiments, he finally designed the Holland VI submarine in 1896. After successfully developing the first practical and effective submarine, he received more orders from the US Government. Thanks to Holland's early contributions, the US Army was able to develop sophisticated weapons, which had a huge impact on the course of the First World War. The Holland VI became the prototype for all modern submarines and Holland became known as the father of the modern submarine. The submarine was not his only invention; he is also responsible for the screw propeller, the hydrocarbon engine, the submarine gun and the auto-drive mechanism.

OUTLAWS

The US Government gradually moved its frontier westward from the 1630s onwards. It considered this the manifest destiny of the US – to expand their territory as far as the westernmost part of the landmass in order to acquire the whole continent. During the time when the Wild West was not yet on the map and the west of the country in general was considered a mystery, quite a few adventurous Irish people moved there and made a living as cowboys, saloon workers, soldiers and so-called outlaws. Many of the infamous out-laws who robbed banks, trains and stagecoaches bore Irish surnames and became an important part in the creation of the myths of the west.

One such legendary figure with a rebellious streak was Billy the Kid (1859-1881). The teenage outlaw of the south-west was born to Irish famine immigrants in the slums of New York City. His real name was William Henry McCarty and he later used the name William Henry Bonney. His mother was desperate to escape the squalor and hardship of New York and give her children better opportunities in life. Shortly after the civil war, they headed west and initially came to Silver City in New Mexico in search of a new life. While singing Irish folk songs with a bunch of Irish immigrants as they crossed the vast landscape, young Billy had to learn how to survive the hard life of western pioneers.

As the life was equally tough in New Mexico, it wasn't long before his mother died of tuberculosis and his stepfather abandoned him. Billy was desperate to scrape together a living from the barren landscape and needed to hustle for money in this strange land. His first killing was supposed to have been in self-defence, but it seems that trouble always found him. The blonde-haired, blue-eyed, intel-ligent and charming outlaw was on the run since the age of 16 and soon became the most wanted man in the region. He was eventually captured and hanged for murder. According to legend, this teenage gunman, also known as the Robin Hood of New Mexico, killed nearly thirty individuals.

NATIVISM MOVEMENT

During the nineteenth century, nativism was rife in American society. Protestant nativists believed immigrants would, among other things, destroy republican values. They were a major threat to the Irish Catholic population in the US. For instance, the Know Nothing movement became active in various American cities around the time when the famine refugees were flooding into America. Their goal was to purify American politics by refusing to accept Catholic immigrants and they wished to favour the interests of established residents over those of newcomers. They were called the Know Nothings because the organisation was secret and when they were asked what their activities were, they simply answered 'I know nothing'.

One of the most significant incidents in this conflict was the Philadelphia Nativist Riots, also known as the Philadelphia Prayer Riots. These were a series of riots that took place in 1844. One of the frustrations that Catholic immigrants had was that their children were being forced to read the Protestant King James Version of the Bible in public school every day. Their requests for them to read the Catholic Bible, along with other demands, were largely ignored and eventually the fracas they caused escalated into huge riots. Nativists targeted Irish Catholic churches and Irish Catholics attacked Protestant churches. The Protestant-dominated Philadelphia city government did not help much and both sides accused each other of starting the fresh outbreak of fighting.

Consequently, signs and notices with messages such as 'No Irish Need Apply', known as NINA, came to be seen throughout the city on shop windows and in newspaper advertisements. Although there was an abundance of jobs if you were not too picky, it was more difficult to find a place to live. The land of the free was initially a far cry from the American Dream. Many people in Ireland actually believed that the streets in the US were paved with gold but in fact it was the Irish immigrants who had to pave them under atrocious working and living conditions, not to mention the widespread discrimination and prejudice they experienced.

The majority of Catholic Irish were fed up with the life on the East Coast. Feeling stifled and frustrated, many ambitious and adventurous young people moved to the south, further west or elsewhere. Some moved gradually with construction work, such as digging canals and laying train tracks, while the others went to California directly, dreaming of striking it rich, especially during the time of the California Gold Rush.

BOSTON

Boston was initially established by Protestant immigrants; however, overwhelming numbers of Irish Catholics started settling in the city as soon as they got off the boat during the famine period and it soon became known as the Irish Catholic city. As had been the case elsewhere, the Irish migrants were often lacking education, skills or capital, so they quickly formed Irish ghettos. But Irish immigrants eventually climbed to power and retained a political monopoly for many decades because of their huge contribution to the city, as well as the large population of Irish descent.

The prominent Father John McElroy (1782-1877) was born in Enniskillen, County Fermanagh. After emigrating to the US, he joined the Society of Jesus and became a Jesuit. He served as an army chaplain during the Mexican-American War. After spending a lot of time educating the Catholic community in Frederick, Maryland, the bishop of Boston, John Bernard Fitzpatrick sent him to work as pastor of St Mary's parish in Boston in 1847. This was a time when public schools in Boston were growing increasingly hostile towards Irish Catholic newcomers and there was a need in the Irish Catholic community for their own place of study, so McElroy established a college, which was the forerunner of Boston College.

James Michael Curley (1874-1958) was a popular Boston politician who served as a Democratic mayor of Boston and governor of Massachusetts. He was born in Roxbury, Boston, which has a high concentration of Irish people. His parents were from County Galway.

The most internationally well-known Irish American is no doubt John Fitzgerald Kennedy (1917-1963). Born in Brookline, west of Boston, he became the thirty-fifth president of the USA and the first Catholic Irish American to be elected president. It was seen as quite an achievement to have an Irish-Catholic person as president by the Irish American population in the country and he became an inspiring role model for many. As president, he famously said of the country of his ancestors in 1963 that:

> This has never been a rich or powerful country, and yet since earliest times, its influence on the world has been rich and powerful. No larger

nation did more to keep Christianity and Western culture alive in their darkest centuries. No larger nation did more to spark the cause of independence in America, indeed, around the world. And no larger nation has ever provided the world with more literary and artistic genius.

The Fitzgeralds came from County Limerick and the Kennedys were from County Wexford. Both families emigrated to the US during the Great Famine. Arriving as destitute immigrants, they made a living as peddlers, coopers and general labourers. The next generations moved up the social ladder and joined the middle classes, working as clerks, tavern owners and retailers. His grandfather, John 'Honey Fitz' Fitzgerald, became the mayor of Boston and a member of the US Congress. Finally, Joseph Patrick Kennedy, John F. Kennedy's father, became a versatile businessman and politician and Rose Elizabeth Fitzgerald, his mother, was a philanthropist.

After studying at Harvard College, John F. Kennedy joined the US Navy and eventually served as a commander in the South Pacific during the Second World War. Upon returning, Kennedy, who was a Democrat, became involved in politics and served in the US Senate. He was only 43 years old when he defeated Republican candidate Richard Nixon in the presidential election of 1960. When Kennedy visited New Ross, County Wexford, in 1963 as president of the United States, he said to the excited crowd:

> When my great grandfather left here to become a cooper in East Boston, he carried nothing with him except two things: a strong religious faith and a strong desire for liberty. I am glad to say that all of his great-grand-children have valued that inheritance.

John F. Kennedy International Airport in New York has since been named in his honour and countless other places, streets, institutions and buildings bearing his name can be found not just in Boston but everywhere in the world.

Another equally inspiring figure of Irish descent was General Edward Lawrence Logan (1875-1939), who was born in south Boston to a family from Ballygar, County Galway. After attending Harvard University, he enlisted in the 9th Infantry of the

Massachusetts Volunteer Militia and steadily rose through the ranks. As a commander, he led troops in the Spanish-American War and the First World War. Logan also worked as a lawyer, municipal judge and was president of several charitable institutions. Boston's Logan International Airport was named after him.

NEW YORK

In the wake of the famine refugees who emigrated in the mid-nineteenth century, waves of Irish continued to arrive at the port of New York. As was the case in Boston, impoverished, uneducated immigrants typically formed slums and shanty towns in no time. According to the US census, by 1880, a third of New York's population was Irish. To cater for growing immigration from Europe, Ellis Island officially opened as a federal immigration station in 1892. The first immigrant to pass through Ellis Island was a 15-year-old girl from County Cork called Annie Moore. She boarded the ship SS *Nevada* with her brothers Anthony and Phillip to join their parents, who had settled in New York. As one of 148 passengers on the ship, she spent twelve days at sea and arrived on New Year's Day of 1892. As the first person to enter the station, she was given the $10 gold coin – no doubt the largest sum of money she had ever seen in her life.

The Irish migrants tended to stick together and several areas of New York became known as Irish neighbourhoods, such as the south-eastern end of what is now Central Park which was called Pigtown as it was here that many people used to rear pigs. In addition, there was the area called Seneca Village, where there was also a large population of black people, and there were high concentrations of Irish people farther north and west. Five Points, in the central lower area of Manhattan, was a well-known Irish neighbourhood in the 1850s. Known as the first slum in America, this was the area to which countless famine refugees flocked after landing on American soil. It was packed with people and full of problems, such as the spread of disease, child mortality, unemployment, crime, fighting and prostitution. Common diseases included cholera, measles, diphtheria and typhus – the death rates were highest among young children, who would have been most prone to disease. Most of the Irish immigrants in the area lived in crammed box rooms and sewage and cattle ran freely in the streets. However, the majority of the people were not gangsters as one might be led to believe by the popular Hollywood film, *The Gangs of New York*, though other aspects of the film might be more true to the reality at the time. Many of the immigrants tried hard to get on their feet and do the right thing, but they struggled to climb higher than the bottom rung of the social ladder – which often took a couple of generations to achieve.

In these atrocious living conditions, it is believed that tap dancing was invented by a fusion of Irish and African traditions. Although not all aspects of Irish culture survived due to the fact that rural immigrants were busy adjusting to the urban American lifestyle, Irish music was resilient enough to persevere. Fiddlers, pipers, flautists, accordionists and Gaelic singers were hired to work in the dance halls, pubs, on the vaudeville circuit, as well as at private functions and special seasonal events and so on. In 1892, the 'Golden Age of Irish Music' was formally declared in the New York City's Celtic Hall and by the turn of the century, the city had become the epicentre of Irish music.

Irish people often lived near their local Irish church and developed their own communities. There was a church called St Lawrence O'Toole Roman Catholic church (currently the church of St Ignatius Loyola) in Yorkville which was built in 1851. The parish's first pastor was the Revd Eugene O'Reilly, who had come directly from Ireland.

Scared of their powerful presence, nativists threatened and tried to suppress Catholic immigrants whenever they could. One of the high-profile secret nativist organisations, the Know Nothings, was a powerful force in New York. Tensions mounted between the swelling number of Irish Catholic and native-born Protestant residents. In 1844, large-scale demonstrations were carried out by Protestants in the Irish areas of New York City. They carried anti-Catholic banners and threatened to burn down the old St Patrick's Cathedral.

Considering their status at the bottom of the social ladder, it is no surprise that Irish Catholics accounted for more than half of admissions to the New York almshouse. They also represented a higher percentage of people admitted to lunatic asylums, charity hospitals and prisons than other social groups and they had the highest rates of cholera, typhoid and typhus due to their overcrowded and unhygienic living conditions.

As parents struggled, their children bore the brunt of the circumstances. Countless orphaned and homeless children slept rough all over New York City in cardboard boxes, sewer pipes or alleyways. Between 1853 and 1929, two charities, the New York Foundling Hospital and the Children's Aid Society, transported up to 600,000 street children – many of whom were Irish – from New York City to foster homes mainly in the Midwest. In different circumstances, Irish nuns sold 2,000 babies born to unwed mothers in Ireland to American families during the 1950s and 1960s.

New York City was the focal point of the American trade union movement, which was mainly controlled by Protestant unionists before the 1830s. Although they were latecomers to the city, Catholic Irish immigrants were steadily catching up with the movement, inspired by their first-hand experience of social injustice back home. As a result, half of the union leaders were Irish Catholic by the 1860s. As many of them were great speakers, conversationalists and organisers with a sense of responsibility, a significant number of them became efficient trade unionists wherever they immigrated.

Tammany Hall, also known as the Tammany Society, was established as a Democratic Party political organisation in New York in 1786. With the society's support, Andrew Jackson's presidential victory was achieved in 1828. It continued to expand its association with the Democratic Party. During the 1850s, it firmly gained political control and more votes as it earned the loyalty of immigrants by helping them find jobs, accommodation and even helping them get American citizenship.

Supported by hundreds of thousands of famine immigrants, the society also helped Irish immigrants move up the political ladder until around the mid-1960s. The relationship was reciprocal.

Historically, Catholic Irish immigrants had mostly been Democrats in the US. Politicians were aware that considerable numbers of Irish immigrants made up the backbone of the society. Getting their support, as well as that of the Catholic Church, was absolutely key. The Tammany Society eventually became a hugely influential institution that had close relationships with saloon keepers and gang leaders. It more or less controlled the saloons, which were indispensable to politicians, who used them for meetings, assembly district organisations, trade legions, essential political activities and various other campaigns. The powerful institution successfully mixed politics, business and pleasure.

Another prominent institution worth mentioning is St John's College, the first Catholic institution for higher education in the region. It was set up by the Right Revd John Hughes (1797-1864) from County Tyrone. He became archbishop of New York and was the most famous Catholic bishop in the US as he served during a period of massive growth in the Catholic population of the country. Hughes' Jesuit university became Fordham University in 1907.

RMS *TITANIC*

A gigantic British passenger liner, RMS *Titanic*, was designed by Thomas Andrews from County Down and built at the Harland and Wolff shipyard in Belfast. After hitting an iceberg just off the coast of Newfoundland on 15 April 1912, it sank in the Atlantic Ocean on its maiden voyage from Southampton, England, via Queenstown (present-day Cobh) in Ireland, to New York City. The death toll was over 1,500, which included 110 Irish people. Andrews was one of those who went down with the boat.

Fifty-four Irish people survived the ordeal. One of the survivors was Jesuit Father Francis M. Browne who got on the ship in Belfast to take pictures of the maiden voyage and got off in Queenstown. An engine room worker, John Coffey, originally from Queenstown, was also lucky to escape as he also disembarked in Queenstown.

CHICAGO

Compared to New York, Boston and Philadelphia, Chicago is a relatively new city. People started settling in the area from the 1800s
onwards. As a result, the anti-Catholic British system was not firmly
established when the Irish arrived in droves. With fewer obstacles to
the realisation of their dreams, they had a genuine opportunity to be
part of the growth of Chicago from its earliest days.

In the 1860s it became the US city with the fourth-largest population of Irish people. Many immigrants initially came via the East
Coast to build infrastructure such as the Illinois and Michigan Canal
in the 1830s. In the beginning, many of them lived in impoverished
areas, working in low-skilled jobs to make a living. (One of those
Irish neighbourhoods was where the Great Chicago Fire of 1871
started – in the barn of Irish immigrants Patrick and Catherine
O'Leary.) The English-speaking Irish had an advantage over immigrants from non-English-speaking countries when it came to getting
into all kinds of industries and before long Irish immigrants moved
from the realm of poverty and unskilled manual labour to the middle
class. They soon established themselves by working in educational
institutions, police and fire departments, and governmental organisations. This was accompanied by a significant change in their living
conditions, many of them going on to own fine houses. By the turn
of the twentieth century, it is estimated that there were 300,000 Irish
and Irish Americans living in the city.

Chicago had a large number of Protestants but the overwhelming majority of immigrants were Catholics. As has been the case in
many places, Catholic priests and nuns played an influential role
in the lives of Irish immigrants and Irish Americans. They were
responsible for building scores of educational institutions, hospitals and schools. The city's first institution of higher education, the
University of St Mary of the Lake, was founded by Bishop William
J. Quarter (1806-1848), who became the first bishop of Chicago
in 1846. Born in Killurin, County Offaly, he came to the US as a
missionary. At the request of Bishop Quarter, the Sisters of Mercy
founded the St Francis Xavier Academy for Females in 1846. The
Sisters of Mercy were responsible for building various institutions

but this was the first Mercy college ever opened in the world. The academy later became St Xavier University.

Religious academic institutions, such as Barat College, Mundelein College, Loyola University, DePaul University and Dominican University, were all built by Catholic communities, led by scores of Irish priests and nuns who oversaw the creation and early development of such institutions and later took up teaching positions in the institutions.

As Chicago was a young city, countless Irish workers were involved in building their own churches, hospitals and schools. Mercy Hospital and Medical Center was built in 1852 as the first chartered hospital in Chicago. Due to the huge demand, it soon started training medical practitioners in its own Lind Medical School and the hospital became the first Catholic hospital. All of this went rather smoothly as most of the early Catholic bishops in Chicago were Irish or Irish Americans. The children of Irish immigrants grew up attending church services and Catholic schools. Irish cultural activities and organisations, such as the GAA and the Gaelic League, also thrived in Chicago. This favourable environment allowed them to retain their ethnic identity relatively easily.

Chicago is one of the American cities where the Irish Republican Brotherhood, or the Fenian movement, flourished in the late nineteenth century. Irish immigrants who became relatively wealthy and successful provided a substantial amount of money, as well as manpower, for the Irish cause. Irish Americans were also active in local politics and Chicago produced a few Irish American mayors over the course of its history. As in other American cities, the Irish typically dominated the Democratic Party.

Although Edward Henry 'Butch' O'Hare (1914-1943) was born in St Louis, Missouri, Chicago's O'Hare International Airport was named after him to honour the great Irish-American fighter pilot. When his parents got divorced, his father – a lawyer who dealt with Al Capone – moved to Chicago. He had a remarkable military career, despite its brevity. As Naval Lieutenant Commander, he led various missions. During the Second World War, his plane was shot down during the night attack over the Pacific Ocean. His body was never found. In 1963, shortly before his own death, John F. Kennedy laid a wreath in honour of O'Hare at the Chicago airport during a ceremony there.

Riverdance sensation Michael Flatley (1958-) was born in Chicago to Irish parents and grew up surrounded by Irish culture. The former world Irish dance champion created and first performed *Riverdance* during the Eurovision Song Contest in Dublin in 1994. *Riverdance* is a theatrical show that was inspired by Irish step dancing and Irish folk music and traditional Irish music instruments such as uillean pipes and fiddles. Over the years, this now globally renowned dance has evolved into a full-length stage show based on the story of the journey of Irish people to the New World.

BUTTE

The little mining town of Butte, Montana, was an ideal place for immigrants in the early 1870s. Newcomers could easily settle down and create their own lives in Butte as it had none of the pre-existing communities and conditions present in other US cities of the East Coast. The only time you would be looked down upon was when you were lazy and didn't work. The bulk of Irish immigrants were experienced miners who arrived from the Beara Peninsula in Ireland. Before arriving in Butte some had also worked at the mines of Comstock Lode in Nevada, the coalfields in Pennsylvania, the copper mines in Michigan and there were even some who had done mining work in Australia.

Immigrants from all across the world came to Butte but it was the Irish who felt the strongest pull. By 1900, the population of Butte was just over 47,000, about 12,000 of which were Irish migrants or their descendants.

The regional airport in Butte is called Bert Mooney Airport. Mooney was a notable Irish American aviator from Butte.

SAN FRANCISCO

After gold was found in north California in 1848, waves of people travelled there by both land and sea on routes that often proved deadly. The city of San Francisco was created by gold-rush pioneers – an adventurous, risk-taking and curious bunch of people who wanted to get a second chance in life. Prior to arriving, almost all the Irish who went to California from the other parts of North America had been disillusioned. Travelling to San Francisco, the city nearest the gold field, was definitely for those with a strong spirit of get-up-and-go.

However, once they made it to the city, San Francisco was a breath of fresh air for many. Although originally only a sleepy little fishing village, everybody who came to San Francisco came with a dream: to become rich and successful as quickly as possible. As a result, San Francisco quickly grew. In the absence of the British, the Irish had an advantage as they were the first immigrant group to settle en masse when the California regions were still part of Mexico and had no established rules or regulations. As the first comers, the Irish promptly became movers and shakers in the city, which they effectively controlled in the early days. They planned the city layout, built roads, churches, schools and hospitals, and thrived as the dominant population group. In the same way that the Vikings built Dublin and the Romans founded London, San Francisco was chiefly established as a city by the Irish. They became the figureheads of the California dream and developed a positive Californian mentality.

A tradition of celebrating St Patrick's Day began in San Francisco in 1852, long before there were paved streets on which to parade. Irish ghettos and slums never existed in San Francisco and nor did 'No Irish Need Apply' signs. Unlike in other American cities, Irish immigrants became the ruling middle class almost immediately in San Francisco. As they were the ones who built the streets, institutions, towns and so on, they were also the ones who named them upon completion and many of them were given Irish names.

The first mayor of San Francisco was Scots-Irish American John White Geary (1819-1873). In 1867, Longford man Frank McCoppin became the first Catholic Irish native mayor in San Francisco and in the US – thirteen years ahead of New York's William Russell Grace and eighteen years prior to Boston's Hugh O'Brien, who became the first Irish-born Catholic mayors in their cities.

Although she didn't stay too long, Lola Montez (1821?-1861) was one of the most unforgettable Irish visitors to San Francisco as she took the mostly male residents of San Francisco by storm.

A true actress, she led a mysterious life by inventing an identity for herself and little is known about the real Lola. She was born Marie Dolores Eliza Rosanna Gilbert, possibly in County Sligo or Limerick. The beautiful brunette was probably ahead of her time in many ways. She first became a 'Spanish' dancer in London and then a courtesan in Paris. Shortly after meeting King Ludwig I of Bavaria, she became his mistress and was made Countess of Landsfeld in Munich. As she did not know how to handle power and wealth, she was kicked out of the country not long afterwards during the revolutions of 1848. After travelling all over Europe, she came to San Francisco, where she performed her famous erotic Spider Dance at night. She briefly went to Australia but local audiences gave her a cold reception, so she returned to the US and spent the rest of her life in New York, where she died quietly at a relatively young age.

During the Gold Rush era, a notorious red-light district called the Barbary Coast was established by a group of criminals from Australia, many of them bearing Irish surnames. The lawless city's early underworld consisted mostly of brothels and gambling houses, which thrived and became the epicentres of vice – banditry, murder, opium smoking, alcohol-induced crime sprees and 'shanghaiing' (kidnapping people to work on ships).

Around the turn of the twentieth century, San Francisco was fully developed and before long, Los Angeles overtook it to become the biggest city in California. Unlike San Francisco, which is on the tip of a peninsula, Los Angeles had huge potential for expansion as it was surrounded by vast areas of land.

The Irish continued to be the main players in Southern California. There was a huge presence of Irish and Irish American actors, actresses, filmmakers and scriptwriters in the Hollywood film industry. By taking over Tinseltown, the Irish inspired and gave hope to ordinary Americans who wanted to escape from reality, particularly during the Great Depression. It was in this way that the Irish won American hearts. Anti-Catholicism, anti-Irish sentiment and many other negative stereotypes from the past were left behind.

Prior to his presidency, Ronald Reagan (1911-2004) began his career as an actor in Hollywood, appearing in nearly twenty films before he joined the US Army. Born in Tampico, Illinois, his great-grandfather arrived in the US from County Tipperary. Just like John F. Kennedy, he gave a rather emotional homecoming speech in the town of Ballyporeen, County Tipperary, in 1984:

> I can't think of a place on the planet I would rather claim as my roots more than Ballyporeen, County Tipperary. My great-grandfather left here in a time of stress, seeking to better himself and his family. From what I'm told, we were a poor family. But my ancestors took with them a treasure, an indomitable spirit that was cultivated in the rich soil of this country. And today I come back to you as a descendant of people who are buried here in paupers' graves.

He is considered the most Jacksonian president since Andrew Jackson himself.

IRISH ORGANISATIONS

Throughout the course of history, a considerable number of secret societies existed in Ireland to counterbalance the inequality of land-lord law, other land usages and socioeconomic practices against Catholic people.

When Irish people moved to the US, the problem of inequality did not go away. It was a different country, but the same British system. One of the most high-profile Irish/Irish-American secret societies in the US was the Molly Maguires. Very rural and Gaelic in nature, this fraternal society was originally formed in Ireland and shortly spread to cities in Britain. Molly Maguires in the US developed into a kind of offspring group and shared the same ideology in a different framework. In the context of the US, Mollies – as its members were called – were coal miners in the anthracite coalfields of Pennsylvania.

The coalfields were controlled by mighty financial syndicates by the 1870s. They recruited hundreds of thousands of immigrant workers, including large numbers of underage children who were willing to work for cheap wages in atrocious conditions. Between the 1840s and the 1860s, approximately 20,000 Irish people worked in Schuylkill County. With no safety regulations, hundreds of serious injuries and deaths occurred every year. The lives of the workers were considered to be disposable. Irish coal miners were treated as second-class citizens and they remained underprivileged, backward and impoverished in the coal regions of the Pennsylvania counties. As a result, many joined the Molly Maguires. Its activities remained clandestine and its members were bound to each other by oath. It was typically an underground movement of powerless working-class Irish labourers whose aim was to fight against greedy yet powerful industrial forces. As a desperate measure, they used force and violence to fight the injustice and Mollies were accused of arson, kidnapping and murder.

To collect evidence to crush the society, James McParlan, also known as James McKenna, from County Armagh, was hired by the Pinkerton National Detective Agency to investigate the Mollies. It took McParlan nearly five years to become a member, gain respect and disclose the inner workings of the society. As a result of the arrests and trials from 1876 to 1878, twenty Mollies were executed by hanging.

The Molly Maguires has been strongly associated with the Ancient Order of Hibernians (AOH), which was formed in New York in 1836. AOH has its roots in the Defenders, a Catholic agrarian secret society that was established in the 1780s in County Armagh. It was initially started as a defensive group in response to the failure of the authorities to take action against raids by the Protestant during the period of the Penal Laws. But it evolved to take on a more political dimension and were involved in the 1798 Rebellion. Eventually, the organisation developed into a group called the Ribbon Society, which was created in opposition to the Orange Order. Ribbonism was a popular movement in the nineteenth century in Ireland and was represented by various associations under different names. Rural Catholic members, such as tenant farmers and tradesmen who lived in appalling conditions under unfair laws, were called Ribbonmen as they wore a green ribbon in their buttonhole. The agrarian secret society members gathered together against landlords and their agents, who were often Protestant. Scores of similar groups sprang up during the hard times in particular. Irish people carried these ideological beliefs with them when they moved to new places.

THE IRA

There were a couple of small-scale famines in Ireland prior to the 1850s but it was the Great Famine that had such a devastating effect on Irish society and, as a result, a considerable impact on human migration at the time. From that time onwards, the majority of Irish emigrants to America were rural Catholics from the south. Between 1846 and 1851 alone, more than a million people left Ireland and the majority of them ended up in the US.

Just as the Catholic Irish had been poorly treated in Britain and Ireland, they had a hard time in the US initially too as the system there was much like the old British system in which anti-Irish sentiment, as well as anti-Catholicism, were deeply rooted. The majority of Irish immigrants lacked education, capital and skills and they usually settled in the poorer districts, often in congested urban environments, which made them more vulnerable, though it also created fertile breeding grounds for nationalism.

Irish people considered their misfortunes – the Great Famine was one of many – to have been caused by mismanagement by the British, so many people who lost family members and had to leave home to survive harboured grudges against the old enemy. This animosity was passed on from generation to generation and was eventually responsible for successful fundraising and support for republican organisations. This widespread support in America played an essential part in the Irish struggle for independence.

Sinn Féin, which means 'We Ourselves', is an Irish republican political party that was established in 1905 with the goal of ending British rule in the whole of Ireland and establishing a united republic.

Many organisations aimed to protect Irish peasants and the rights of Catholics. The IRA originated from the Irish Volunteers who fought during the Easter Rising in 1916. It was founded to end British rule in Ireland and later fought for the reunification of Ireland. The Northern Ireland conflict has never been simply

Protestant versus Catholic; it is much more complex than that and the religious differences are woven into a story of English oppression and Irish resistance that has been going on for centuries.

The US Government had been reluctant to get involved with The Troubles as it was viewed as an internal problem of Britain. Since the 1970s, the British and Irish Governments desperately sought to end financial contributions to the IRA that came from Irish immigrants or their descendants in the US. Margaret Thatcher became the British prime minister in 1979 and adamantly treated the Northern Ireland affair as a domestic issue by putting IRA members in prison as common criminals rather than political prisoners. The Clinton administration's political intervention moved things forward. Irish republican politician Gerry Adams has been visiting the US since 1994 thanks to the visa that was issued to him by Clinton and the talks conducted under the auspices of the American president helped advance the peace process. As a great supporter of the peace process, Clinton visited London, Belfast, Derry and Dublin in November 1995, thus becoming the first US president to visit Northern Ireland. He was far more committed to the intractable problems in Northern Ireland than any of his predecessors. Two and a half years after his visit, the Good Friday Agreement was signed. This ended direct British rule and officially brought about an IRA ceasefire, although isolated violent incidents still occur.

COUNTY ASSOCIATIONS

County Associations exist all around the globe but they have their origins in the US. In the nineteenth century, once you got on the ship and crossed the Atlantic Ocean, you didn't get to see your home or loved ones again. That's why the tradition of an American wake started, which was a living wake or a sombre version of send-off party at which people said their last goodbyes to those who were emigrating to America. After starting a new life in the US, County Associations functioned as a lifeline during this transition or mourning period.

Some of the first associations were established in New York since the 1840s. Most of the immigrants were rural people who had never even been outside of their village and suddenly found themselves alone in urban areas. With their own chaplain, county Associations acted like a family by giving a sense of belonging and community to those who were homesick. Each association organised social and cultural events such as GAA games, Gaelic language/music events, dinner dances and Communion breakfasts, as well as benevolent assistance to help fellow county people. Members were well looked after by their association, especially when they got sick or when somebody died. When times were tough, it was essentially the place to go to have a good time, hear the familiar accent, speak the same language, catch up on news from home, find jobs and accommodation, and meet new friends – or even future husbands or wives.

LABOUR UNIONS

The labour union (trade union in the UK) is a by-product of the Industrial Revolution and Catholic Irish people were traditionally involved in the union movement wherever they settled. Mistreated and underpaid workers formed the first labour unions, although they were more like fraternal organisations in the beginning. To form a union, effective leadership and management skills are essential. With their affinity for politics, the Irish became the prominent arbiters of American labour unions. Some of the biggest railroad unions were the Brotherhood of Locomotive Engineers (founded in 1863), the Order of Railway Conductors (1868), the Brotherhood of Locomotive Firemen (1873) and the Brotherhood of Railroad Trainmen (1883).

The Knights of Labour was established in 1869. This high-profile organisation eventually developed a typical working-class culture, including women and families, and organising leisure and educational activities for its members. One of the most successful railroad strikes, the Great Southwest Strike, was organised by the Knights of Labour in 1886. It was the most powerful conflict between management and organised labour and it involved more than 600,000 workers shutting down railway lines in five states – Arkansas, Illinois, Kansas, Texas and Missouri.

Strikes organised by labour unions were regular occurrences by the 1880s. Between 1881 and 1905, there were nearly 40,000 strikes, mainly led by construction workers and coal miners. In 1881, the Federation of Organized Trades and Labour Unions was established to encourage the formation of trade unions.

One of the most distinguished labour leaders was Julia Sarsfield O'Connor Parker (1890-1972), who significantly improved women's rights. Born in Woburn, Massachusetts, the daughter of Irish immigrants, she started off working as a telephone operator and eventually became a remarkable labour leader. She was president of the National Women's Trade Union League (WTUL) Boston office and head of the National Telephone Operators' Department of the International Brotherhood of Electrical Workers (IBEW). As president, she demanded higher wages from the New England Telephone Company as operators' wages were a third lower than those of people working in manufacturing. She successfully organised the strike in 1919 when approximately 9,000 female operators in New England succeeded in shutting down most of the telephone service. A settlement was agreed after a couple of days and she started campaigning to improve women's rights on a national level. She carried on working after marrying Charles Austin Parker, a reporter for the *Boston Herald*.

Affectionately known as Mother Jones, Mary Harris Jones (1837-1930) was a hugely influential labour organiser who changed the course of the labour movement history in the US. She dedicated her life to improving the lives of miners and child workers. Born into a Catholic family in County Cork, she emigrated to Canada before settling in the US. A schoolteacher and dressmaker by profession, there were two major turning points in her life: firstly, she lost her husband and all four children to yellow fever in Memphis, and secondly, after moving to Chicago for a fresh start following a tragedy, she lost everything she owned in a fire, including her lifeline – her dressmaking workshop.

She had to start off again from nothing. After joining the Knights of Labour, a forerunner of the Industrial Workers of the World, brave

Mother Jones worked tirelessly to improve mine workers' lives. As she successfully led strikers and helped their families, her opposition called her 'the most dangerous woman in America' and 'grandmother of all agitators'. In the same way, she encouraged all people to join the union, worked to improve the work environments of child workers and tried to change the child labour law. She went as far as risking her own life to improve their working conditions. She was arrested, detained, faced charges of libel, slander and sedition, but never gave up what she had started. She died at the age of 93 and is buried in the Union Miners' Cemetery in Mount Olive, Illinois, where many miners – or 'my boys' as she used to call them – who died of strike-related violence were laid to rest. Various places and institutions have been named after her, including *Mother Jones* magazine, a left-wing American magazine which covers politics, the environment and human rights.

ST PATRICK'S DAY

One of the most accessible and conspicuous global celebrations is probably St Patrick's Day. Although St Patrick's Day had been observed from around the tenth century, it was an Irish Franciscan friar from County Waterford, Luke Wadding (1588-1657), who made it a feast day. Irish immigrants and Irish Americans have been celebrating it since the eighteenth century in the US, long before it was first organised in Ireland and before the US Declaration of Independence. Today celebrating St Patrick's Day is an official government event in the US.

Early celebrations largely grew up out of immigrants' longing for Ireland and Irish nationalism by uniting against British rule. During the mid-nineteenth century, Catholic priests openly preached nationalist themes on St Patrick's Day, such as British oppression and suffering to churchgoers, many of whom would have been famine immigrants. The collective celebrations gradually helped make the Irish diaspora proud of their country of origin.

The first ever St Patrick's Day celebration was held by the Charitable Irish Society of Boston in 1737. As the organisers were Scots-Irish, it was simply a way of honouring Ireland; the people gathered at a service of worship which was followed by a dinner.

The first gathering was held in New York on 17 March in 1762. Irish soldiers in the British Army in New York led the inaugural parade in 1766. George Washington allow his troops in the Continental Army a holiday on 17 March in 1780 'as an act of solidarity with the Irish in their fight for independence'. US cities where such celebrations were established before the twentieth century include: Boston (in 1737), New York (1762), Philadelphia (1771), Morristown (1780), New Orleans (1809), Buffalo (1881), Savannah (1824), Carbondale (1833), New Haven (1842), Milwaukee (1843), Chicago (1843), Saint Paul (1851), San Francisco (1852), Atlanta (1858), Scranton (1862), Cleveland (1867), Pittsburgh (1869), Kansas City (1873) and Butte (1882).

In modern times, to celebrate Ireland and Irishness, as well as to maintain links with Irish communities abroad, the Taoiseach, or Irish prime minister, usually visits the US and his ministers attend events all across the world, from New Zealand to Mexico. People celebrate everything Irish, and the festivities include religious observances, parades, dances, music, Guinness, Irish food, Gaelic language and sports events.

The shamrock ceremony originally started on 17 March in 1952 when the first Irish Ambassador to the US, John Joseph Hearne, visited the White House to wish President Harry Truman, who was of Irish descent, a happy St Patrick's Day. (Truman was known for attending the St Patrick's Day parade in New York in 1948. He was the first president to do so – taking the obscure ethnic ceremony to a whole new level.) As Truman was out of office, Hearne left a gift of a box of Irish shamrocks. Since then, the US president receives a cluster of shamrocks every year. Hearne was not just being friendly; the move was politically motivated as the nascent Irish Republic was neutral during the Second World War and in 1952 was not yet a member of the United Nations nor part of NATO yet. It therefore had few official allies. He informally wanted to highlight the presence of the Irish diaspora in the US, and probably hint at the importance of Irish-American votes for the president, in order to encourage friendly relations between the US and Ireland. Today US presidents visit Ireland every four years, even those leaders with no Irish ancestral connections, because Catholic votes – in particular Irish Catholic votes – still count for a great deal in the US. A visit to the emerald isle might be politically motivated but with their mutual interests, respect and trust, the two countries' special relationship is undeniably solid.

SPORTS

The Irish played a big part in the development of American sports. For instance, professional baseball was firmly established during the 1860s, which was around the time the children of the famine immigrants grew up and started playing serious sports. Irish players were the backbone of popular teams such as the Hartford Dark Blue, the Middletown Mansfields, the Boston Americans (changed to the Boston Red Sox), the Boston Red Caps, the Boston Braves, the Boston Beaneaters, the Boston Reds, the Chicago White Stockings (the original club of the Chicago White Sox and the Chicago Cubs), the Troy Trojans, the Washington Nationals, the New York Giants (changed to the San Francisco Giants), the New York Mutuals, the Buffalo Bisons, the Baltimore Orioles, the Cleveland Forest Citys, the Rockford Forest Citys, the Pittsburgh Pirates, the Athletic Club of Philadelphia (now the Oakland Athletics), the Philadelphia Athletics (also known as the Athletic Baseball Club of Philadelphia), the Philadelphia White Stockings, the Cincinnati Kelly's Killers, the Cincinnati Reds, the Allegheny (the current Pittsburg Pirates), the Louisville Grays, the Detroit Tigers, the Brooklyn Atlantics (the current Los Angeles Dodgers), the St Louis Brown Stockings (now the St Louis Cardinals), the Houston Buffaloes (originally the minor league developed into developed into the Houston Astros), the Fort Wayne Kekiongas, and the list goes on.

A countless number of Irish and Irish American players, umpires and managers have been enshrined in the Baseball Hall of Fame in Cooperstown, New York. Irish Americans were the dominant players until around the turn of the century.

BANKS

The bank functioned as the most important part of an immigrant's settling-down process. Without a bank, immigrants couldn't have bought a house, saved money or even looked to the future. The oldest savings bank in New York City was the Emigrant Savings Bank, which was founded in 1850 by the Irish Emigrant Society members. The Hibernia Savings and Loan Society (HSLS) was also established by Irish immigrants in 1859 in San Francisco. HSLS was responsible for the high levels of home ownership among Irish immigrants in the city.

3

CANADA

The fact that the US had been such a popular destination for the Irish doesn't mean its next-door neighbour was a blind spot in the history of Irish migration. In fact, between 1825 and 1970, more than 1.2 million Irish people migrated to Canada and by 1867 they accounted for 24 per cent of the country's population, making them the second largest ethnic group after the French. According to the national census conducted in 1931, approximately a third were Catholic while two-thirds were Protestant Irish immigrants.

Throughout the nineteenth century, the number of newcomers fluctuated depending on the price of a transatlantic passage. More people arrived in Canada when fares to Canadian ports were cheaper. It was not uncommon for the Irish to go to Canada in order to continue on to the US. Although life in the US was equally challenging, for better or for worse, there were more opportunities and the family ties in the US were undeniably solid.

Although the overwhelming majority of famine migrants ended up in the US, Canada also received a great number. With little or no accommodation, the new arrivals had to house themselves in sheds in the waterfront slums and many later ended up in the poorhouse, the almshouse or the infirmary. The sudden influx of Irish immigrants changed the culture of the region and a plethora of Irish towns, street and place names, and people with Irish surnames are scattered all across the country.

NEWFOUNDLAND

Irish people have long had a special relationship with Newfoundland. The distance between Ireland and Newfoundland is approximately 2,060 miles (3,300 kilometres). Located on the east coast, it is the closest territory to Ireland where St Patrick's Day is a national holiday. It is the most Irish place in Canada, with more than 50 per cent of Newfoundlanders claiming Irish ancestry.

According to the early historical record, Ireland's first connection with Newfoundland was through trade. By the sixteenth century ships regularly travelled from Ireland loaded with butter, pork, salted beef and tallow, which they exchanged for fish and cod liver oil. One such ship, recorded in 1536, was *Mighel* (Michael) from Kinsale, Cork. The trade in fish lead the Irish to affectionately refer to Newfoundland as Talamh an Éisc – Land of the Fish.

In the early eighteenth century, the next big wave of visitors came from Counties Waterford and Wexford and worked there as regular seasonal immigrant workers. They primarily worked in the fisheries in the summer and went back home in the autumn. Many of them, however, became permanent settlers. For those who were Irish or of Irish descent in St John's, a well-established support system existed. This included the Benevolent Irish Society (BIS) which was established as a philanthropic organisation in 1806, it is the oldest philanthropic organisation in North America.

After the War of 1812, the Irish population had doubled and included a sizeable number of native Gaelic speakers. Newfoundland today has its own distinct dialect, which includes many phrases based on Gaelic and the Irish accent is well preserved.

During the late eighteenth century, Orangeism became a rising force in the Newfoundland population. As alarmed local authorities put various restrictions on the endless stream of Catholic immigrants, they started leaving Newfoundland for Nova Scotia, Cape Breton and New Brunswick with their fishing and other businesses.

NOVA SCOTIA

In 1621, Scotsman William Alexander named Nova Scotia, which means 'New Scotland' in Latin, and the region was briefly ruled by the Scottish. Some of the early settler groups were Presbyterian Ulster-Scottish and Catholic Irish seasonal workers. The first big wave arrived in the late 1750s and they settled in Guysborough County. In Erinville, Salmon River Lake and Ogden today, Irish surnames are ubiquitous and the accent, music and food are all distinctively Irish. Many people initially came from counties Londonderry, Donegal, Tyrone and Antrim. One of the earliest Irish organisations, the Charitable Irish Society, was founded in 1786 in Halifax.

The next large wave of immigrants arrived between 1815 and 1845 and came from counties Wexford, Waterford, Kilkenny, Tipperrary, Kerry and Cork. By this time, Halifax and Dartmouth had become the major settlements and Irish immigrants accounted for almost half of the population in the two communities. As many of them were fishermen and tradesmen, the government provided free land so the men could make a living as farmers. When there was a construction boom (for example, when the railways were being built), the majority of them joined the workforce as navvies.

One of the most famous Irish immigrants is Revd William Sommerville (1800-1878) from County Down. He arrived in Canada as an ordained missionary and established the Reformed Presbytery of New Brunswick and Nova Scotia in 1832. He later became minister of the West Cornwallis congregation in Grafton, Nova Scotia in 1833.

Sir John Sparrow David Thompson (1845-1894) was prime minister of Canada between 1892 and 1894. Born in Halifax, the capital of Nova Scotia, to a Waterford-born father and a Scottish mother, he worked as a lawyer before getting into politics. He was the fourth prime minister of Canada and the first Roman Catholic prime minister.

NEW BRUNSWICK

Ireland and New Brunswick have a lot in common geographically. As well as their similar shape, size and landscape, they both have inland waterways, a coastline and large tracts of bogland. The capital, Saint John, contained a considerable number of Irish immigrants but New Brunswick's most Irish region was the Miramichi region where there was a surge of capable and skilled immigrants at a time when it was relatively easy to travel to this part of New Brunswick on empty timber cargo vessels because they stopped in Ireland on the way back to Chatham and Newcastle. They found temporary work in the timber trade upon arriving and soon secured land grants. As a timber-exporting colony, New Brunswick provided plenty of business opportunities.

This part of Canada was initially settled on agricultural lands around the river valleys of Miramichi, Saint John and Kennebecasis, but life here was as arduous as it was in Ireland. One of the peak periods of Irish immigration was between 1830 and 1835, when passage from Ireland to the US cost £5 whereas the cost of a ticket to Canada was £3 or even £2. Fertile and viable land was limited and taken by earlier settlers and most of the area was not suitable for agriculture, but Irish immigrants in the nineteenth century clung tenaciously to farm life. Some of those who arrived genuinely wanted to start a new life in Canada, while others took advantage of the cheaper passage to cross the Atlantic to Canada as a way of getting to the US (New Brunswick shares a border with the US state of Maine). Some of the reasons for staying in Canada included: a lack of money preventing them from travel further; large land grants offered to people at relatively affordable prices; family members already settled locally. But the fact is that the majority of immigrants couldn't see a future in New Brunswick and ended up emigrating from there to other Canadian cities or neighbouring US states, such as Maine, New Hampshire and Massachusetts. It is estimated that only 25 per cent of Irish people who arrived in New Brunswick settled there.

QUEBEC

The Irish were the single largest ethnic group in Quebec and Ontario long before the Great Famine. The majority of them sailed to Quebec from the English city of Liverpool. The St Patrick's Day celebrations in Montreal first started in 1824 and the shamrock is featured on the municipal flag of Montreal.

During the famine period, hundreds of thousands of people, including orphans, arrived on Grosse Île, which was a quarantine station for the port of Quebec. They had to go through a medical examination here to make sure they were free of disease before entering the country, but large numbers of the weak and starved immigrants who arrived on the coffin ships were infected with typhus and other diseases. In 1847 alone, nearly 100,000 passengers left for Canada but more than 5,000 people died at sea. Further, 5,424 people were buried at Grosse Île, also known as Île des Irelandais, making it the largest burial ground for famine victims outside Ireland. Because of the intensity of the location, a Celtic memorial was later erected there. More people were buried at mass burial sites in surrounding areas. Those immigrants who passed the medical examination were sent to Montreal and the already large Irish community there grew significantly larger. At one point, nearly half of Quebeckers had Irish ancestry. The majority of Irish immigrants worked as navvies, building infrastructure in Montreal, such as the Victoria Bridge.

An outbreak of typhus, which is also known as ship fever, hit the region in 1847, killing approximately 6,000 people, in the wake of which a significant number of Irish people formed their own communities in rural and urban regions of Quebec.

As the Irish population grew, they built their own churches, hospitals and schools. St Patrick's Basilica was opened on 17 March in 1847. Loyola College was established by the Jesuits for Irish Catholic people in 1896.

One of the most high-profile Irish immigrants in Montreal was Thomas D'Arcy McGee (1825-1868). Born in Carlingford, County Louth, he was a gifted speaker, journalist, poet and politician. After being involved in the Young Ireland movement and the Irish rebellion of 1848, he ended up emigrating to the US, before settling in Montreal where he edited and wrote newspaper articles about Irish and Canadian politics. He entered the political sphere and eventually became the Minister of Agriculture, Immigration and Statistics in the conservative government. McGee was called the Father of Confederation as he dreamed of forming a new nationality through the unification of British North America. He played a key role in advocating educational rights for minority Catholics. But towards the end of his life, he became critical of Irish republicanism and many people treated him as a traitor. In 1868, he was shot in the head by Patrick James Whelan and died instantly. It is widely believed that this assassination was a Fenian plot but the truth of this has been buried in history.

ONTARIO

The first big wave of Irish emigration to Ontario occurred during the early nineteenth century. The Irish people who arrived in the 1820s were predominantly missionaries and soldiers. Thousands of famine refugees arrived via nearby Grosse Île and local nurses, doctors, nuns and priests all helped the destitute newcomers. By 1851, the Irish were the biggest ethnic group in Toronto, the capital of Ontario.

As was the case elsewhere, Irish women worked as domestic servants while the men became navvies who helped to turn Toronto into a vibrant, growing city. Major construction work done with the help of Irish workers included the Rideau Canal, which was opened in 1832. Hundreds of navvies died of malaria while working on the canal.

To attract settlers, land grants were awarded in many places, such as in North Hastings County, meaning that vast swathes of land were relatively affordable. The huge tide of immigrants who arrived, notably from counties Tipperary and Cork, scattered across many different areas and established their own settlements. However, the development of new industrial cities nearby was to prove irresistible during a time of expansion for the nascent country and many Irish immigrants abandoned their colonies for those flourishing localities with the result that scores of once dynamic settlements disappeared or turned into ghost towns.

Toronto had an equal number of Catholic and Protestant Irish immigrants. They often fought each other – skirmishes and riots occurred regularly but not to the same degree as in American and English cities where Catholic immigrants experienced institutionalised racism, discrimination and prejudice. Irish immigrants, both Catholic and Protestant, were among those most likely to own homes by the turn of the twentieth century in Ontario.

One notable Irish emigrant to Canada revolutionised modern business practices. Timothy Eaton (1834-1907) was born in Ballymena, County Antrim. He arrived in Ontario at the age of 20 with a 100 pounds in his pocket. His little dry goods store opened in Toronto in 1869 and became the foundation of the Eaton's department store. It eventually developed into one of the largest department stores in America as Eaton revolutionised business practices by selling items for cash at a fixed price, offering satisfaction or money refunded, and reaching small towns and rural communities thanks to mail-order catalogues.

Born in Enniskillen, Ontario, Robert Samuel McLaughlin (1871-1972) founded the McLaughlin Carriage Company, the forerunner of General Motors of Canada. Robert's grandfather, John McLaughlin, was originally from County Tyrone. In 1832, he and 140 other Irish people arrived in Canada having been persuaded to come by a Canadian agent looking to populate the Peterborough area. (During the 1800s, various schemes both governmental and private existed to populate certain localities.) Robert had started work in his father's carriage manufacturing business as an upholsterer. He established the McLaughlin Carriage Works in Oshawa with his father and brother George. His family business turned into the McLaughlin Motor Car Company and was later purchased by General Motors. With McLaughlin as president, General Motors of Canada expanded rapidly and the Oshawa plant had 3,000 employees by the mid-1920s.

ORANGE ORDER

First-generation Irish immigrants generally have high levels of political awareness because of their bitter first-hand experience and the complicated history of their homeland. Large numbers of Irish in Canada were involved in political activism, regardless of their social background; both Protestant and Catholic Irish were actively involved in politics.

The best-known Irish institution in Canada is the Orange Order. According to the 1871 census, more than 60 per cent of Irish immigrants were Protestant. Canada has a deep Protestant tradition.

The Orange Order has been operating since the early 1800s and it has played a significant role in Canadian history. Early members were exclusively from Ireland but it soon embraced other Canadian Protestants, such as the English, the Scottish, the Italians and even the Mohawk local Americans who joined the order and bonded with Irishmen. During its peak, one in three of Canada's Protestant adult males were members.

In Newfoundland, the majority of Irish Catholic settlers were pre-famine immigrants and so had had many years to found businesses and prosper. As a result, many were wealthier than Protestant immigrants. This motivated the newly arrived Protestants to join the Orange Order to protect their interests. For instance, St John's native union leader and politician, William Ford Coaker (1871-1938), established the Fisherman's Protective Union at the Orange Hall in Herring Neck in 1908. This exclusively Protestant union also functioned as a political party.

The Orange Order peaked around 1920 and became particularly powerful in Ontario and Newfoundland. Local Orange Lodges served various functions, acting as mutual benefit societies, social clubs, recruitment agencies, as well as hosting cultural events, such as dancing, music and parades. In 1920, about 35 per cent of adult Protestant men in Newfoundland were Orangemen. Newfoundland has a strong Orange jurisdiction which is similar to Ulster border counties. The majority of mayors in Toronto have traditionally been Orange members. Toronto became so 'Orange' at one stage, it was called the Belfast of Canada.

A unique feature of the Irish in Canada is that they functioned as an indispensable bridge between the French and the British – sharing religion with the French, and language and history with the British. There have been tensions between Protestant and Catholic

Irish immigrants for as long as they have co-existed, but they were at least united against the French.

IRISH NATIONALISM

Immediately after the American Civil War, Irish and Irish-American veterans tried to capture Canada as a hostage in order to secure Ireland's independence from British rule. This Fenian invasion of Canada occurred five times between 1866 and 1871. Although the Fenians defeated a Canadian force at Ridgeway, their attempts mostly failed.

Despite the fact that the country was full of Irish people, Irish nationalism didn't take root in Canada the way it did on US soil. Some of the reasons were: there were proportionately more Protestant immigrants in Canada; Canadian cities' Protestant strong-holds were relatively small in size, less contentious and didn't have a history or a tradition of repressing Catholic people. As well as this, Catholics in the US mostly settled in urban areas while their counterparts in Canada settled in remote rural areas, which made it hard to stir up political agitation. Catholics in the US quite often hovered at the bottom of the social ladder for more than one genera-tion while the immigrants in Canada were more economically and socially secure, which allowed them to put their past behind them and move on. Irish-American nationalism generally stemmed from the obstacles met living in America. There was not enough breeding ground for Irish nationalism to take root in Canadian soil. Unlike the East Coast of the US, there were no established or authorita-tive Protestant strongholds in Canada and, as a result, Irish Protestant and Catholic people simply integrated into Canadian society and became Canadians rather than Irish immigrants living in Canada.

Canada did, however, have an influence of the Irish Home Rule movement. Irish Home Rulers saw Canada as a model for increased Irish autonomy within the British Empire. British prime minister William Gladstone's draft of the first Home Rule Bill in 1886 was based on the Canadian model – the British North America Act of 1867, which formed the Confederation.

TRADE UNIONS

Quite often, Irish immigrants from Britain and US brought their trade unions with them when they travelled abroad. During the nineteenth century, trade unions started mushrooming – both locally grown unions and Canadian branches of international trade unions. The early legal details and legislation were copied from British unions and later the Canadian framework merged with US legislation. For instance, the Amalgamated Society of Engineers (ASE), the first Canadian branch of a British union, opened in Montreal in 1853. Other unions with headquarters in the US were the National Union of Iron Moulders (established in 1859), the Locomotive Engineers (1864), the Typographical Union (1865), the Knights of St Crispin (1868), the Cigar Makers (1869), the Bricklayers and Masons (1872), the Locomotive Firemen (1876), the Knights of Labour (1879), the Railway Conductors (1881), the American Brotherhood of Carpenters (1882), the Railroad Trainmen (1885) and the Painters and Decorators (1887). When times were bad in their locality, trade unionists typically moved with their unions between countries in the hope of finding work elsewhere.

Elizabeth Flynn Rogers (1847-1939) was known for her inspiring union activities. Born in Ireland during the peak of the famine, she arrived in London, Ontario, in 1854 via New York. She went to school in London but her parents couldn't pay for schooling so she had to start working as a tailor at 17. She married George Rodgers, a labour organiser and avid women's rights advocate. Her serious trade unionist career started when she joined the Knights of Labour. She was among the first women who were actively involved with the struggle for workers' rights. She dedicated her life to improving women's and men's rights and eventually became a leader of the Knights of Labour. As she had first-hand experience of unfair treatment, she was a natural choice as a leader to work for underprivileged people. After leaving the Knights of Labour, she joined the Catholic Order of Foresters and worked to secure women's death benefits and insurance premiums. She and her husband had to move a lot in the 1870s as they were blacklisted by local authorities. She strongly believed men and women should be paid equally and have the same rights.

Trade union leader Daniel John O'Donoghue (1844-1907) was another prominent historical figure. Born in Listry, County Kerry, he migrated to Canada with his family. He had to work as a printer from the age of 13 due to the death of his father. He moved to New York and joined the National Typographical Union. After living in several US cities, he came back to Ottawa and helped to organise various unions such as the Ottawa Typographical Union, the Ottawa Trades Council and the Trades and Labour Congress of Canada. He was eventually chosen to work for the newly formed Department of Labour because of his enormous contribution to the labour movement. He is considered a major founder of organised labour in Canada.

EDUCATION

The Irish also contributed to education by developing a system of mass education – a set of school textbooks called the Irish National Readers – in Canada. The majority of pupils in Ontario, Quebec and the Atlantic provinces were taught using the school curriculum, which had been imported directly from Ireland. The Irish National Readers, which featured Bible stories, animal stories and poems, was extremely popular and described by some as the best series of elementary school texts in the nineteenth-century English-speaking world.

HOCKEY

There has been a huge debate over whether hockey, Canada's national sport, has its roots in hurling. Considering their similarity, it is certainly likely that there is an element of hurling in the evolution of hockey. Hurling is the oldest sport in Ireland and has been played since ancient times. The Irish had been settling in Newfoundland since the fifteenth century and youngsters from County Waterford, and then Kilkenny, Wexford and Cork, were certainly playing their native sport on Canadian soil, whether on the ice or field. Some early Canadian pictures show that hockey sticks were once almost identical to hurleys, or hurling sticks, suggesting that there may be a link between the two sports.

4

The Caribbean

Although it may not be immediately evident, the Irish connection to the Caribbean is quite strong and it has a long, tangled history. Hundreds of thousands of Irish were shipped to the region as slaves during the ethnic cleansing and genocide instigated by English authorities in the sixteenth and seventeenth century. Irish slavery could be called a forgotten part of the history of slavery, as it was already well established long before the advent of the transatlantic African slave trade.

The sixteenth century was a turbulent period in Ireland. English kings wanted to convert Catholic Irish people to Protestantism, as they had successfully done in Wales and Scotland. The Plantations of Ireland had therefore started and the Penal Laws of the English Government – a series of disadvantage laws imposed on Irish Catholics – were in full swing. The planting of English Protestant settlers in Ulster and Munster on confiscated Catholic land had bloody consequences as the English regime clashed with the Gaelic lords.

In order to 'root out the Papists and fill Ireland with Protestants', King James I of England encouraged the sale of Irish political prisoners to the New World. Under the reign of James II, Charles I and Oliver Cromwell, the ethnic cleansing of Ireland was more systematically carried out. Beginning with Irish Catholic priests, who were the biggest target, hundreds of thousands of ordinary people were killed by sword or disease. Some took refuge by fleeing to Catholic countries in Europe, such as France and Spain. From the early 1600s, many were captured for various reasons and sold as slaves to plantation owners and settlers in the New World – the Caribbean as well as North American British colonies, such as Carolina, Virginia, Maryland and New England.

During Cromwell's conquest of Ireland, or the Irish Confederate Wars (1641–1652), it is estimated that Ireland lost about a third of its population. The impact of Cromwell's population transfers was devastating. 'To hell or Connaught' was the saying of the day, which gave people the choice of either being killed or moving to the barren lands across the River Shannon where it was impossible to make a reasonable living. They were also shipped in large numbers across the Atlantic to the Caribbean. Their only crime was being Catholic.

The English authorities also used the islands as a dumping ground for undesirables such as vagrants, petty criminals, widows and orphans. After being sent there, many women and girls were forced to work as prostitutes.

The British are normally meticulous record keepers, but we do not know how detailed the notes on this atrocity were as the Public Record Office of Ireland lost almost all its records when it was destroyed by an explosion and the resulting fire during the Civil War in 1922. No former slaves who survived the ordeal told their own stories either. Due to the nature of the business, it is hard to estimate the exact number of settlers, but it is believed that up to 400,000 Irish slaves were shipped like cattle during the seventeenth century to work on cotton, sugar and tobacco plantations. As a result, the Caribbean islands were full of Irish slaves, especially in the 1650s, which was the peak decade of Irish slavery. They were scattered all across the region and could be found in Montserrat, Antigua, Barbuda, Barbados, Bermuda, Jamaica, St Lucia, St Kitts and Nevis, Trinidad, St Vincent, Grenada, Guiana and Haiti. There were more Irish slaves in the Caribbean than any other ethnic group until African slaves arrived in droves.

Although some slaves had generous masters and built prosperous, or at least reasonable, futures upon attaining freedom, the treatment of the vast majority of Irish slaves was atrociously inhumane most of the time. If they tried to escape, they were branded FT, or fugitive traitor, on the forehead. They were whipped, beaten until they bled, strung up by the hands and their feet were set on fire as punishment. African slaves had to be purchased as they were considered an investment, but Irish slaves were more or less disposable and Irish slaves were bought much cheaper – sometimes they were almost free – and treated worse than African slaves.

To increase assets, Irish slave girls were forced to interbreed with African male slaves as mulatto slaves could fetch more money than pure Irish slaves. This allowed buyers to spend less rather than purchasing new African slaves. This practice of producing slaves for sale became so widespread that legislation had to be brought in to ban mating Irish slave women with African slave men.

The British Parliament abolished the transatlantic slave trade in 1807. As soon as they had the chance, many former slaves and servants moved to the US or elsewhere in search of better life. Some runaway slaves became pirates in the Caribbean.

The Irish have not always been the casualties of history. Although the majority of them were victims, a fair number of Irish people made a fortune from the slave trade as plantation owners, slavers, slave-ship captains, as well as indirectly being involved with the slave business as forced transportation became a way of life in Ireland and the Caribbean. They were typically both the exploiters and the exploited.

A group of second-generation Irish settlers in particular became ambitious slave traders, buying slaves from British or French ships. For example, a Westmeath immigrant's son, Nicholas Tuite, successfully imported slaves to the newly developed island of St Croix by reallocating slaves from Montserrat. Due to his hard work, the numbers of slaves reached more than 20,000 and sugar exports also substantially increased by 1773. With seven plantations, he became one of the wealthiest slave traders.

Along with the main English slave ports of Bristol, London and Liverpool, some ports in Ireland also played a crucial part in the slave trade, which created various employment opportunities. Cork, Limerick and Belfast prospered during the eighteenth century by exporting manufactured goods such as guns, irons, cloth, salty and pickled products and importing sugar, tobacco, cotton and rum. Dozens of established slave-trading companies and traders who dealt with both Irish and Africans were listed in those ports. Irish ships eventually started sailing directly from Africa to the Caribbean. Some of the leading figures who made huge profits from the slave trade included John Roche and the Creaghs from Limerick. Irish merchants Thomas Greg and Waddell Cunningham from Belfast also made a fortune. Greg, Cunningham & Co. was once the most powerful trading house. They initially dealt with Irish potatoes, butter and beef, and, after establishing Irish, West Indian and US trade connections, they moved on to a more lucrative commodity: slaves.

MONTSERRAT

It was Christopher Columbus who visited the island in 1493 and named it after the mountain abbey in Spain. After the conquest of Ireland by Cromwell at the siege of Drogheda in 1649, Montserrat became the primary destination for Irish slaves, although the Irish had been transported there as early as 1632. The first group of Irish people came to the island from St Kitts, which became the first English colony in the region in 1624.

Affectionately called the 'Emerald Isle of the Pacific', Montserrat remains the most Irish place in the Caribbean – St Patrick's Day is even a national holiday on the island. Among hundreds of thousands of Irish slave workers, there were large numbers of Gaelic speakers. Current residents of the island are mostly black, but they are the descendants of both Irish and African slaves. Their accent and expressions derive from the way Irish people used to speak – the most conspicuous feature being the Connacht accent.

During the height of the European slave trade, approximately 70 per cent of the Montserrat population was Irish. By the eighteenth century, African slaves became more conspicuous and widespread, replacing Irish slaves. During this time, scores of people with Irish surnames such as Lynch, Roach, Hussey, Daly and Farrell owned African slaves. Today the region is filled with Irish place names and many of the locals have Irish surnames either because they are actually descended from Irish people or because their ancestors took on the names of their Irish masters. Eventually slaves, masters, merchants and ordinary settlers all blended together in society.

Irish and African slaves had to live and work together but they usually didn't get on well at all. In terms of the climate there, African slaves were better suited than the Irish, who had no experience of the heat of the tropics. It was more than 3,000 miles (4,830km) away from home – the scorching equatorial sun burnt Irish people's fair-skinned legs, which gave rise to the word 'red leg'. 'Redlegs' became a derogatory term for powerless Irish people. The population of the Redlegs dwindled as the majority of them left the islands and settled elsewhere but quite a few of them remained under atrocious conditions. The Redleg minority are still present to this day, 400 years later, and they live in their own small community, maintaining their culture and identity. Although conditions have improved for them, they still remain somewhat underprivileged in terms of land ownership, job opportunities and the various consequences suffered due to inter-family marriage.

BERMUDA

This British Overseas Territory is located in the North Atlantic Ocean, just off the east coast of the US, and it has been used as an important strategic military base. The island was first discovered by the Spanish, then English colonists heading for Virginia were shipwrecked there in 1609 and ended up settling on the island. Thousands of Irish people were sent here during Cromwell's rule.

In the nineteenth century, the Royal Navy bought 200 acres on Ireland Island, which is the north-westernmost island, and built a naval base, dockyard and lighthouse there. Many political prisoners from the Young Irelander Rebellion of 1848 were shipped here to join the convict labour force to develop the dockyard and naval base. One of the most high-profile political prisoners was the Irish nationalist activist and politician John Mitchel (1815-1875). A leading member of Young Ireland, he was arrested in 1848 and sent to the prison in the Caribbean. Along with hundreds of thousands of other prisoners, he survived life on the prison hulk, brutal living and working conditions, yellow fever and other diseases, not to mention the prison revolts that occurred sporadically.

Another well-known resident was the Irish poet Thomas Moore (1779-1852). He was appointed registrar to the Admiralty in Bermuda in 1803. But he only stayed here briefly as he found the tropical life boring and uninspiring. During the Anglo-Boer War, a substantial number of Boer prisoners of wars were also transferred to Bermuda from South Africa.

Other islands in the Caribbean also received a substantial number of Irish slaves. For instance, approximately 25,000 Irish slaves were present on St Kitts and Nevis by 1650, and there were also Irish slaves in Jamaica, where a couple of thousand Irish slaves were sent during the same period.

5

SOUTH AMERICA

There are three main features about Irish migrants who travelled to South America.

Firstly, the most visible group was the Irish in the armed services. Some arrived as soldiers and officers on British or Spanish frigates. Britain and Spain were the major colonial forces in the region before the newly formed nations became independent. Spanish kings traditionally trusted the Irish and treated them as their cousins. Later Irish soldiers also joined the local liberation armies and played a major role in the fight for independence of most Spanish colonies in South America. With plenty of exceptional army and navy officers, Irish settlers established and developed the local armed forces. Consequently, former officers became politicians when peace returned to the countries and made up part of the foundation of many South American cities and towns.

Then, there were the settlers who came with dreams of having their own land and became farmers. The Irish typically worked in the sheep-farming business in the beginning and, after saving up money, purchased their own land tracts. The people who settled in the early 1800s were not the most desperate and impoverished immigrants as the passage didn't come cheaply due to the long voyage and the infrequency of the ships bound for South America. Most of them simply couldn't inherit land back home because they were not the first-born son. They typically crossed the Irish Sea first and went to Liverpool, England, where they got on a boat that would take them to South America. The journey took more than a month. As there were vast spaces of land to cultivate, successful Irish immigrants often invited their relations to join them. During the eighteenth and nineteenth century some migrants moved to South American countries with the aid of the Spanish Government who helped Catholics escape English oppression.

The last noticeable characteristic of the Irish in South America is that they were the dominant middle- and upper-class people. This was because, in most cases, they had already established themselves as qualified or experienced workers by the time they arrived in their adopted country. Early Irish immigrants in this region were mainly from well-off families, which meant they were relatively well-educated and skilled professional people.

Irish settlers were actively involved in commerce, medicine, literature and religion, especially during the eighteenth-century Spanish Enlightenment period. Without encountering prejudice and discrimination, those Irish with valuable skills or qualities reached high positions quickly.

ARGENTINA

The most popular destination for the Irish in South America was Argentina, which is currently ranked as the fifth-largest Irish community in the world and the largest in a non-English speaking country. It is estimated that up to a million Irish descendants are living there.

Some of the first Irish people to set foot on Argentine soil were crew members of the 1492 expedition of Christopher Columbus. When Columbus first visited the Galway port, which was a thriving trading port in those days and a common stop for Spanish ships, Columbus became acquainted with some local Irishmen who ended up joining him on his expedition.

The Portuguese explorer Ferdinand Magellan's circumnavigation of the world (1519-1522) also involved a few Irish sailors. The cabin boys, brothers William and John, known as Guillermo and

Juan, from County Galway got on a boat with Magellan, who served the Spanish king. His ship had a crew of eighteen men and visited Argentina in 1520.

The majority of early settlers came from the Midlands, notably counties Wexford, Westmeath, Longford and Offaly. As these Irish pioneers, especially merchants, became successfully established, they invited their relatives to settle too. During the 1820s alone, more than 7,500 Irish people came, either directly from Ireland, or via the USA, Canada and even Australia. Some of the early settlers were Protestants but the bulk of them were Catholic.

As Argentina is not an English-speaking country, the early Irish immigrants tried to integrate by changing their names. Many people started using a Spanish first name and some even changed their surname. Typical names include: Rodolfo Walsh, Ricardo Murphy, Santiago Phelan. Some immigrants even changed their surname. For instance, the surname O'Brien became Obregón.

One of the primary reasons for moving to such a faraway country was that they could be landowners for a relatively affordable price. This was a great incentive, despite the physical and psychological distance. Many migrants also used Argentina as a base and later settled in neighbouring countries, such as Uruguay, Paraguay, Brazil and Chile, when better opportunities arose there.

The Farrel brothers, John and Thomas, came to Argentina and settled there in 1536. They initially came along with Pedro de Mendoza, the Spanish explorer who conquered the *Río de la Plata*, or the River Plate, which is the river on the border between Argentina and Uruguay, and claimed it for Spain. Future settlers brought cattle, sheep, pigs and horses, which was probably the first time such animals had been seen on Argentine soil. The animals adapted very well to a new environment and prospered in the Pampas.

Some of the popular destinations for the people who settled in the countryside were the littoral provinces where many of them typically worked as cattle dealers, shepherds and farmers. In fact, Irish immigrants were responsible for the world-famous quality Argentine beef. A couple of hundred skilled workers from Ireland, such as salters, butchers and tanners, arrived in the late eighteenth century when more than 20,000 African slaves were brought into the country to work in the Argentine beef industry. Irish immigrants Peter Sheridan and George Dowdall established the first meat-packing house in the country.

Many Irish immigrants who started off as farmers built good lives in Argentina. Thomas Duggan (1827-1913) from Ballymahon, County Longford, came to Buenos Aires with his family. They all started working as sheep farmers and their business became enormously successful very quickly. The family soon became successful wool merchants and landowners. Thomas invested in land in San Antonio de Areco and other places – in total 300,000 hectares of the best land – as well as banks, mines, cattle ranches, railways, immigration services and the press, not only in Argentina but in Uruguay as well. He is believed to have been one of the wealthiest Irish immigrants in South America in the late nineteenth century. He was not just a rich man but a staunch Irish nationalist who gave back to society as a member of the local education board and an active member of the local Catholic Church community.

One of the earliest contributions in the field of medicine was by Clare man Michael O'Gorman (1749-1819). He was the founder of the first medical school in Buenos Aires in 1776. After studying in Paris, Reims and London, where he specialised in smallpox, he obtained a medical licence in Madrid. While working with the Spanish Army, he came to the River Plate area to work as the official surgeon on the expedition of the Spanish viceroy Pedro de Ceballos. He quickly started treating smallpox patients, built establishments to isolate contagious patients and introduced vaccinations. After establishing a medical school, he focused on teaching the young and starting various preventive medicine projects. When the Argentine War of Independence broke out, the state physician swiftly made himself useful by tending wounded and sick soldiers.

The early settlers in Argentina, especially around the River Plate area, included a throng of 'Irish Yankees'. Among them was Bernard Kiernan (1780-1863), originally from County Derry. He was a trained surveyor and astronomer and initially migrated to the US. Like many Irish people, he found life on the East Coast of the US unsatisfying and suffocating, so he moved to Argentina and settled in the River Plate area.

As they didn't speak Spanish when they first arrived, Irish settlers worked hard to keep their own community going. In 1830, the first ever brewery in Argentina was established by John Dillon, giving a place for well-settled Irish immigrants to meet and have a good time. The Irish population kept increasing and three-fourths of Buenos Aires' Irish were from County Westmeath around this time. Thomas Armstrong (1797-1875) was partly responsible for the population growth. This talented Offaly man was a landowner, director of the National Bank, the Bank of Buenos Aires Province, and the founder of the Argentine Insurance Company. He was also involved with the construction of railways in various regions. After marrying the daughter of the chief officer under Spanish rule of Buenos Aires, he firmly established his business and political contacts. With the growing economy, Irish entrepreneurs in Buenos Aires recruited dozens of would-be immigrants in Ireland during the 1820s. Armstrong and John Thomond O'Brien were among those who went back to Ireland and recruited 'moral and industrious' immigrants, accompanied by their own chaplain and physician, from Ballymahon, Ballymore and Mullingar, where the Armstrongs were well-known local landlords.

When the dictator Juan Manuel de Rosa, who was partial to British settlement, took control in the 1840s, Irish sheep farmers from Uruguay came in considerable numbers to Buenos Aires to settle. Their main new settlements were in Carmen de Areco, Salto, Pergamino, and later Nueve de Julio and Lincoln.

As was the case in with other groups of Irish immigrants, Irish priests and nuns were the backbone of society and acted as a support system for Irish settlers. They served as teachers, nurses, ministers, matchmakers, as well as founders of their own churches, schools and boarding schools. Without their support, Irish communities couldn't have survived at all. Priests sometimes came first and sometimes after but quite often emigrants and priests made the journey together.

The most notable priest to emigrate to Argentina was a Dominican priest named Anthony Dominic Fahy (1805-1871), from Loughrea, County Galway. As soon as Father Fahy arrived in Argentina, he moved in to Thomas Armstrong's house and stayed there, without paying rent, for the rest of his life. Initially Fahy came to Buenos Aires to replace Father Patrick O'Gorman, and he became a great bonding agent for the Irish community, helping to keep it alive. The versatile priest was an efficient leader and was known to be a great matchmaker within the Irish community, but he also worked as a financial adviser, marriage counsellor, judge, consul and postmaster. He successfully set up the Famine Relief Fund and collected significant amounts of money from the immigrants who had become relatively wealthy. The fact that Armstrong was his banker allowed immigrants to borrow money to purchase land fairly easily. He tried to produce Irish priests locally and at the same time helped bring Irish missionaries such as Father Patrick Joseph Dillon, Father Patrick Lynch, Father Thomas Carolan, Father John Baptist Leahy, Father Thomas Mulleady, Father Felix O'Callaghan and Father Edmund Flannery to Argentina.

By 1900, various Irish religious orders had founded educational institutions in Argentina, such as the Irish College for Girls (established in 1857), St Patrick's College (1861), the Irish College for Boys (1862), St Peter and Paul (1865), St Brendan's (1869), St Joseph's (1872), Holy Faith School (1875), Sacred Heart College (1875), Windsor College (1875), St George's (1876), Nuestra Señora de Luján (1877), St Bridget's Industrial School (1887), Holy Cross College (1881), St Patrick's (1887), Fahy Institute (1891), Mater Misericordiae (1897), St Lucy's (1897), St Bridget's (1899), St Stanislaus (1900) and St Paul's College (1900).

Although many people slowly and gradually integrated into the local population, many Irish immigrants and descendants faithfully kept their own cultural and ethnic identity. People who were educated in Irish schools typically received lessons by priests in English in the morning and in Spanish in the afternoon. There are currently twenty Irish schools in Argentina. Irish children who were educated at an Irish school speak English with a perfect Irish brogue from the Midlands even though they have never been to Ireland.

For newly arrived settlers who needed help, advice and a platform for exchanging information and organising social activities, *The Standard* was established by Dubliner Edward Mulhall in 1861 and the *Southern Cross* newspaper was established in 1875 by Dean

Patricio Dillon, a notable businessman and government official in Buenos Aires. These papers were some of the first English-language newspapers in Argentina.

In the beginning, the *Southern Cross*, the oldest Irish Catholic newspaper established outside of Ireland, was written entirely in English but today 90 per cent is written in Spanish. As one of the longest-running Irish newspapers for immigrants, its continued existence reflects the steadfastness of the local Irish community over the years and there is still a huge demand for it. Nowadays, the third-generation Louis Delaney and the fifth-generation Martin Casey work on the newspaper in the shoebox-sized *Southern Cross* newspaper office in Buenos Aires. There is an old typewriter that was actually used in the early days, a sepia-coloured map of Ireland, black-and-white John F. Kennedy and Éamon de Valera photos are on the walls, the old bookshelves are filled with dog-eared vintage books, and century-old logbooks and early Irish immigrants' detailed information are all kept as if the office were a little museum.

One of the early editors was William Bulfin (1864-1910). Born in Birr, County Offaly, he started editing the *Southern Cross* after emigrating to Argentina. He meticulously observed local society and wrote a book called *The Tales of the Pampas*. He was a staunch nationalist and his children, who were born in Argentina, also inherited his republican outlook. His son took part in the Easter Rising in 1916 with Patrick Pearse and his daughter Catalina married Seán MacBride, republican politician and later president of Ireland. Bulfin was responsible for introducing hurling to Argentina.

There were numerous attempts to encourage more Irish people to come to Argentina. In 1889, Irish agents Buckley O'Meara and John Dillon recruited nearly 2,000 Irish people, mainly in counties Dublin and Cork, and shipped them in the steamer *City of Dresden*. The atrocious conditions on the ship killed scores of people during the three-week voyage. To rub salt in the wound, the plan to establish the Irish Colony of Napostá with their workforce also failed as the land was not suitable for cultivation. This is called the Dresden Affair and its disastrous end put many future Irish migrants off moving to Argentina.

One of the most distinctive features of Irish immigration in this region is that countless Irish people fought for the cause of South American freedom because the Irish identified with their struggle and provided support in the name of a shared Catholic religion. José de San Martín (1778-1850), an Argentine general and the leader of the South America's struggle for independence from the Spanish Empire, had a large number of Irish troops. As happened elsewhere, the Irish often ended up fighting their fellow countrymen. The British Army brought about 25,000 soldiers to the River Plate region to fight against Spain in the early 1800s and most of them were directly recruited from the Midlands of Ireland. After the battle, many stayed in Argentina or Uruguay. Once they settled down, chain migration began.

One of the most accomplished Irish immigrants was Admiral William Brown (1777-1857), also known locally as Guillermo Brown. He was born in Foxford, County Mayo, possibly as an illegitimate child as he took his mother's surname. When he was a child, he emigrated to Philadelphia, Pennsylvania, with his family. From his humble beginnings as a cabin boy in the US Navy, he eventually emigrated and settled in Argentina. He became an owner of a ship and started trading between Buenos Aires and Montevideo. During the Argentine War of Independence, he got involved with military activities in Argentina. After becoming a colonel in the Argentine fleet, he steadily climbed all the way to the top rank.

He is considered one of the country's most important national figures as he fought and led his troops to victory not just in the Argentine War of Independence, but also in the Cisplatine War in Uruguay and the Anglo-French blockade of the *Río de la Plata* as well. As he was the first admiral of the country's maritime forces (the Armada de la República Argentina, or ARA), he is called the father of the Argentine Navy. After retiring from his military duties, he took up farming and he died as the greatest patriot in Argentina in 1857. Nowadays there are statues of him in Argentina, Ireland and beyond. Schools, institutions and streets bearing his name are scattered all over the country, not to mention countless warships and political entities that are also called Brown.

A fellow Mayo man, John King, or Juan King (1800-1857), immediately joined Brown's fledgling navy upon arriving in Argentina.

Born in Newport, County Mayo, he served with distinction under William Brown against Brazil and Uruguay. He became marine sergeant major and one of Brown's most trustworthy captains.

While Brown fought at sea, John Thomond O'Brien (1786–1861) defended on land. This Irish hero, born in Baltinglass, County Wicklow, helped lead Argentina to independence and was the aide-de-camp for José de San Martín. Affectionately called Don Juan O'Brien, he also fought in Chile, Peru and Uruguay and had risen to the rank of colonel by the time of his death.

Up to 50,000 people were estimated to have gone to Argentina in the nineteenth century but nearly half of them left for the US or elsewhere before long. Immigration reached its peak in the 1920s, with those escaping the violence of the War of Independence, or the Anglo-Irish War, and the Irish Civil War. This group of emigrants contained both Catholic and Protestant Irish immigrants who settled in various remote regions, including the Falkland Islands.

The most internationally well-known Argentinian of Irish descent in this region is the revolutionary Che Guevara (1928–1967). Unfortunately he had dropped his Irish surname by the time he became famous but his ancestor, Patrick Lynch, was born in County Galway in 1715. The powerful Lynch family was gradually being pushed from Ireland by the Protestant ascendancy. Patrick left for Catholic Spain and initially stayed in Bilbao but continued on to Argentina before long. After marrying a wealthy local heiress, he accumulated lands and became a powerful landowner in the River Plate area. Many significant Lynches lived between Patrick and Che. Ernesto 'Che' Guevara Lynch was born in Rosario in 1928. His father, also called Ernesto, once made an interesting observation about Che: 'The first thing to note is that in my son's veins flowed the blood of the Irish rebels.'

María Eva Perón (1919–1952) was the First Lady and wife of President Juan Perón. Her maiden name was Duarte, which was probably derived from the common Irish surname Doherty. She grew up in the countryside and her father was a wealthy rancher. Her life features in various films and musicals because of her popularity. The person who introduced Juan Perón into government was Edelmiro Farrell, the de facto president of Argentina between

1944 and 1946. Farrell's grandfather, Matthew Farrell, was born in County Longford and his grandmother was Mónica Ibáñez, which is a Spanish version of the surname Evans.

CHILE

For obvious logistical reasons, settlers arrived in Chile only after stopping over or residing in Argentina or other countries first. Compared to Argentina, Chile has a much smaller population and geographical area, but there are approximately 120,000 Chileans of Irish ancestry. As was the case in Argentina, Galway brothers William and John were the first recorded Irish people to have visited Chile. They were in the country in 1520, although it is unclear how long they stayed there. Captain John Evans, known locally as Juan Ibáñez, came to Chile in 1737 and married a local girl of Spanish ancestry. After becoming a successful trader of livestock, he purchased a large ranch and tracts of land. This Irish settler was a great inspiration as he paved the way for fellow country people. Carlos Ibáñez, who became president of Chile twice, first between 1927 and 1931, then between 1952 and 1958, was his great-great-grandson.

Another Irishman who left a lasting impression in Chile is Ambrosio Bernardo O'Higgins, or Ambrose Bernard O'Higgins (1720-1801), 1st Marquis of Osorno. Born in Ballynary, County Sligo, the O'Higgins became tenant farmers in County Meath after their family lands were confiscated. He came to South America via Spain and worked as a merchant in many of the colonies, such as Venezuela, Peru and Argentina, before arriving in Chile in 1757. He worked for a fellow Irishman, John Garland, a former cadet in the Hibernia Regiment and a cavalry officer of the Military Order of Santiago. Garland was initially sent to Chile as a planning engineer to develop the city of Concepción and later became military governor of Valdivia. O'Higgins was a young engineer-draftsman and working under Garland, who was supervising construction of a road over the Andes. Upon completion, this road made the year-round transport of goods possible for the first time.

With the right abilities and useful engineering skills, O'Higgins naturally became an indispensable figure in the development of the country. Among other things, he was responsible for creating a reliable communications infrastructure. In no time, his talent and ability were noticed by local government officials and he was soon appointed to be a Spanish colonial administrator. Other ranks he held during his career were colonel, cavalry captain, captain general of Chile, governor of Chile and eventually viceroy of Peru. He founded the fort of San Carlos, and built many towns, roads, bridges and schools.

His main focus was on improving local infrastructure at a time when the region was rather primitive and underdeveloped. In order to develop the nascent country, many highly skilled engineers were recruited in Ireland and sent to Chile. A group of engineers from Trinity College Dublin were involved in various projects commissioned by the Spanish Government. Engineers John and Matthew Clark joined the team to develop the trans-Andean railway. Upon O'Higgins' recommendation, fellow Irishman Tomás O'Shee became governor of Coquimbo and La Serena in northern Chile in 1790 and also joined the forces. After serving in the Irish regiment in Spain, O'Shee was quickly promoted to captain. He held quite a few responsible positions, such as commander of the Chiloé Archipelago.

As a man of great foresight, O'Higgins then poured his energy into increasing the local population by inviting more Irish immigrants to come from Argentina. He also recruited soldiers and skilled workers directly from Ireland. Some of them eventually became notable statesmen, including James Glover, John MacKenna, Timothy Cadagan, William Taylor and Charles Emanuel Weber, to name a few – all of them came to Chile thanks to O'Higgins.

One of O'Higgins' remarkable qualities was that he had good communication and interpersonal skills. As a result of trusting relationships established with indigenous Indian tribes, which were often distrustful of the new settlers, he successfully concluded various treaties with them.

The last part of his life was spent as viceroy of Peru in Lima, where he died. He was in charge of a vast region during this time, consisting of modern-day Peru, Chile, Bolivia, north-west Argentina and some western parts of Brazil in 1796.

Ambrosio's illegitimate son, Bernardo O'Higgins (1778-1842), also left glorious footsteps. Although he never met his father, he followed the same path and became a patriot just like his father. He led Chile to its independence from the Spanish Empire and was called the founding father of Chile.

Born in Chillán, he completed his studies in England and spent some time in Spain, before becoming a farmer on a large tract of land in Los Angeles, Chile, which his unknown father had left him. Using his father's resources and connections, he eventually came to work for the Spanish Government. Knowing the right people in the world of politics helped progress his military career. His friendships with Juan Martínez de Roza, the pro-independence leader, and Juan Mackenna, also a hero of the Chilean War of Independence, inspired his political career and life. O'Higgins was involved in various conflicts in the struggle for independence in Chile until it was finally gained on 12 February 1818. After becoming the first Supreme Director of Chile, he created a new government. He was committed to economic and social development, creating the Chilean Navy, and establishing schools, libraries and hospitals, but as a liberal, enthusiastic politician, his reforms were typically met with strong opposition. After being kicked out of the country he ended up, like his father, in Lima, Peru, where he died. As an illegitimate child himself, he also produced an illegitimate son, Pedro Demetrio O'Higgins.

In his honour, plaques, statues and busts were erected and countless towns, streets, institutions and ships in various countries, including Ireland, Spain, England, Argentina, Chile, and even faraway places he had never visited, were named after him. The highest award for a foreign citizen in Chile is also named after him. Despite spending the last part of his life in exile, he was considered the liberator of Chile and is considered one of the most significant historical figures in the history of the country.

O'Higgins had many notable relations. For instance, Thomas O'Higgins, a nephew of Ambrosio, became governor of the Juan Fernández Islands and La Serena and Coquimbo, and mayor of Santiago, after arriving in Chile in 1794.

Accomplished high-profile Irish soldiers and administrators could be found all across the country. Among those who were heavily involved in local affairs was John MacKenna, who was known locally as Juan Mackenna (1771-1814). Born in Clogher, County Tyrone, he served for the Irish regiment in Spain. One of his uncles, Alexander O'Reilly (1728-1794), was also notable as he served in the Spanish Army and later became the father of the Puerto Rican militia and governor of the formerly Spanish Louisiana. O'Reilly commanded the Spanish troops in Africa and, thanks to his remarkable achievements and work ethic, he earned the nobile title of *Conde* O'Reilly. After fighting numerous wars in Europe and Africa, and rising through the ranks, his nephew, John MacKenna, came to Chile in 1796.

Ambrose O'Higgins appointed MacKenna governor of Osorno in southern Chile. He expanded infrastructure, building schools, roads, bridges, store houses and mills, throughout southern Chile, where hundreds of thousands of Irish traders and skilled workers had settled. After marrying a local woman, McKenna firmly put down roots in Chilean soil. He played an essential role in the fight for Chilean independence. He also maintained a good relationship with Ambrose's son, Bernardo O'Higgins, during the War of Independence. He served the first Chilean Government, developed the Chilean Corps of Military Engineers and became governor of Valparaíso in 1811.

Another distinguished Irish soldier was Charles Maria O'Carroll, or Carlos María O'Carrol, who came to Chile in 1818 via England and Spain. He fought in the Napoleonic wars and earned the rank of lieutenant colonel. George O'Brien, or Jorge O'Brien, was captain of the Chilean Navy during the Chilean War of Independence. He died in action and is remembered as a Chilean naval hero.

In the field of medicine, there were some prominent Irish doctors who made a difference to the lives of the Chilean people. William Cunningham Blest (1800-1884), also known as Guillermo Blest, from County Sligo, was a medical doctor of middle-class Protestant origins. With a degree from Trinity College, he first worked in London, before coming to Valparaíso in 1823. After founding the first School of Medicine in Chile and becoming the president of the first Medical Society of Chile, he built dozens of hospitals, cemeteries, orphanages and helped the poor.

Dominic Nevin also played a highly influential role in the medical field. This Irish physician became a professor at the Royal University of San Felipe in Santiago and helped produce countless future doctors.

Britain was trying to secure the trading industry in Valparaáso in 1896, which resulted in the arrival of more than 32,000 British and Irish settlers. Young brothers Frank and Tom Galvin from County Tipperary were among those who arrived in Chile. They both worked as teachers. Frank married Ana Clara Pinochet Vargas, the ancestor of President Augusto Pinochet.

After Chile gained independence in 1810 and Argentina in 1816, many Irish immigrants moved on to different places. Thanks to the Roman Catholic Relief Act, severe restrictions put on Catholics were gradually reduced in Britain and the USA and English-speaking Irish people naturally preferred English-speaking countries as their choice of settlement.

MEXICO

Irish soldiers have a long tradition of serving Catholic countries. In many cases, Catholic Irish people identified themselves as Catholic first and Irish second. Many brave Irish soldiers fought for Catholic Mexico and settled there when the war ended and it is estimated that there are approximately 500,000 people of Irish descent in Mexico.

One of the first Irish people to set foot on Mexican soil was William Lamport (1615-1659), also known as Guillén Lombardo, or Guillén de Lampart. He was born in County Wexford to a Catholic family of seafarers, so it was natural for him to become an adventurer after receiving a Catholic education from Jesuits in Dublin and London. He was arrested while distributing Catholic pamphlets on the streets of London but managed to escape and went to Spain to be a pirate. After serving briefly with Spain's Irish regiment, he was sent to Mexico as a result of a scandalous love affair with a noble-woman in Spain. As the Mexican authorities believed he was a threat to Spain, they executed him. With a nickname of *El Zorro*, or the Fox, and an audacious life riddled with mysterious tales, he became a legend.

The American state of Texas was an integral part of Mexico and was called Mexican Texas between 1821 and 1836. It was Irish immigrants who oversaw the development of Texas from its earliest days. James Power (1788-1852) was born in Ballygarrett, County Wexford, and he came to New Orleans, Louisiana, as a merchant. Upon hearing of the land grant offers, he moved to Saltillo, a north-eastern Mexican city, and became a Mexican citizen. While working for a mining company there, he met a merchant named James Hewetson from County Kilkenny. Along with Irish empresarios Donegal man John McMullen and Sligo man James McGloin, Hewetson and Power helped established the region of Refugio and San Patricio in Texas while it was under Mexican jurisdiction. Working closely with the Mexican Government, Power and Hewetson developed Refugio while McMullen and McGloin were in charge of San Patricio. To populate the area, they encouraged 'Irish Catholic people with a good moral character' to settle there. Power even went back to his hometown of Ballygarrett in 1833 with promises of large plots of land and he brought back around 600 Irish immigrants for his colony in Texas. Unfortunately, before even reaching Texas, quite a few of them died of cholera when they got off the boat in New Orleans. A couple of years after the unfortunate event, Irish Catholic immigrants from County Wexford came en masse and settled in Texas. Power was the person who signed the Texas Declaration of Independence.

During the eighteenth century, the majority of people who represented Spain in Mexico were Irish or of Irish descent. Juan de O'Donojú y O'Ryan, or simply Juan O'Donojú (1762-1821), was the last Spanish ruler of the colony New Spain, which consisted of current Mexico, most Central American countries, some Caribbean islands, the regions of the US west of the Mississippi River and Florida. He was born in Seville, Spain, to Kerry and Tipperary immigrant parents and his surname was originally O'Donohue. He joined the Spanish Army and steadily rose through the ranks. The Spanish Army formed an Irish regiment in Mexico and all officers naturally had Irish surnames such as Barry, Fitzpatrick, O'Brien, O'Leary, Healy and Quinn.

Hugh O'Conor (1732-1779), also known as Hugo Oconór, was born in Dublin. He was the descendant of Turlough Mór O'Conor, high king of Ireland, and was a noble statesman who rejected English rule. Hugh went to Spain to live with his cousins, Alexander and Dominic O'Reilly, who had become officers in the Spanish Royal Army. It was natural for him to join the Spanish Army to serve for New Spain, or the countries under the Spanish Empire. He first developed his military skills in Cuba and Mexico, then became a military governor of northern Mexico and then of Texas. He founded a town of Tucson, Arizona, US. After a steady and distinguished military career, he served as governor of Yucatan Peninsula until he died there.

Hundreds of thousands of Irish soldiers fought for Mexico in the War of Independence. The man who commanded the Irish soldiers was Seán Pádraic Ó Raghallaigh (1817–1850), also known as Jon O'Riley, John Patrick Riley or Juan Reley. He was born in Clifden, County Galway, the son of a tenant farmer from Connemara. Upon joining the British Army, he initially went to Canada in 1843. After moving to Michigan, he joined the US Army and served as a private at a time when large numbers of Irish immigrants were hired by them with promises of good salaries and land after the service. But Riley and his comrades soon deserted the army in considerable numbers due to religious and cultural discrimination. Irish Catholic soldiers were mistreated by nativist officers, their Catholic religion was not recognised and they were forbidden to attend mass. At that stage, most Irish soldiers felt sympathetic towards Catholic Mexico, which was being bullied and harassed by Protestants, as had happened in Ireland and the US. Irish deserters therefore promptly joined the Catholic Mexicans in their fight against the Protestant Americans.

Riley founded the Batallón de San Patricio, or the St Patrick's Battalion, with fellow countryman Patrick Dalton to fight for Mexico. It consisted chiefly of deserters who joined the Mexican Army to fight against the US during the Mexican-American War in 1846. However, it was not just deserters who took Mexico's side – some early Irish settlers living on the West Coast, or present-day California, also joined the cause. At the time, the region was part of Mexico, so some Irish immigrants took Mexican citizenship and joined the military. The Mexicans affectionately called them *los colo-*

rados, or the red-coloured people, as the fearless fighters had reddish, tanned complexions and ginger hair. The battalion comprised of a couple of hundred, mostly Catholic, soldiers. Desperately in need of more soldiers, Mexico gave higher salaries to mercenaries, as well as citizenships and land grants.

During the Mexican–American War, the US Government was determined to expand its borders westward in the spirit of Manifest Destiny. The US was desperate to reach the west coast so that they could secure a major port there. Mexico was the biggest obstacle as it was hampering the American Dream.

Waving their green flag with the harp and the words *Erin go Bragh*, the St Patrick's Battalion fought a handful of battles for Mexico. The first time they officially served as a Mexican-Irish regiment's artillery battery was in the Battle of Monterrey in 1846 with Riley as the commander. Their final combat, the Battle of Churubusco, which took place in Mexico City in 1847, ended in disaster. They fought hard but after losing most soldiers in action, Mexico surrendered. Nearly 100 San Patricios were captured by the US Army and punished as deserters. Being a deserter is a capital offence, so if captured by the US Army, they were tried as traitors and hanged. It is estimated that over 9,000 soldiers from the US Army deserted during the Mexican-American War. Afterwards, mass executions by hanging took place. Riley avoided the severe charge as he had left the US Army before the war. Nevertheless, he was punished by being branded with a letter 'D', for deserter, on his side cheek. He suffered a second humiliation because the executioner burnt the letter upside down the first time, so he ended up being branded on both cheeks. The financially strapped Mexican Government couldn't afford to keep the San Patricio anymore. It was subsequently disbanded and, according to the rumour, Riley disappeared into the countryside. The San Patricio regiment was short-lived but it was nonetheless an important group in the history of Mexico.

When peace arrived, it was time to focus on developing the nation. Irish soldiers were replaced by Irish traders and miners. Newcomers became part of burgeoning communities all across the country, such as in Zacatecas and Guanajuato. Disillusioned by the discrimination and prejudice they suffered upon arrival, scores of famine immigrants who initially settled in US cities such as Boston and New York re-emigrated and ended up in Mexico.

Among well-known Mexicans of Irish descent is Álvaro Obregón (1880-1928), who was president of Mexico between 1920 and 1924. Born in the northern Mexican town of Sonora, he was a former farmer who played a crucial role in the Mexican Revolution (1910-1920). As a skilled negotiator and diplomat, he was known for his trustworthy relationship with local Indians who were often rebellious. Coming from a humble background, he became a great role model for the people.

An internationally distinguished actor, Anthony Quinn (1915-2001), or Antonio Quinn, was born in Chihuahua. His father, Frank Quinn, was an Irish immigrant from County Cork who settled in Mexico. After moving to the US – first El Paso, Texas, and then Los Angeles, California – he became an internationally renowned actor. He eventually became a naturalised US citizen and was the first Mexican American to win an Academy Award in his supporting role in *Viva Zapata!* in 1952. He was a versatile actor who played all kinds of characters, from Italians to Chinese men, and he also painted, wrote books and scripts.

BRAZIL

According to legend, the name 'Brazil' derives from the mythical Hy-Brassil, which was said to be an island of the blessed located to the west of Ireland. Although the Irish presence in Brazil was never significant, some Irish people did trickle into the country over the centuries. In order to fit into the local society, some Irish families translated their surnames into Portuguese. Some typical names were Luise (Lynch), Calehano (Callahan) and Bruno (Brown).

One of the first Irish immigrants who settled in Brazil was Thomas Field (1547-1626), who was born in County Limerick. His father was a medical practitioner. After entering the Jesuit Order in Rome, he came to São Paulo, Brazil, in 1577 as a Society of Jesus missionary. He established missions in many localities and died in

Asunción, Paraguay. He is considered the first Irish priest to serve in South America.

In 1612, the brothers Philip and James Purcell from Ireland established a colony in Tauregue on the Amazon River. They were Anglo-Irish tobacco traders. English, Dutch and French settlements also existed during this period, and a group of Irish slaves were sold to work on tobacco plantations. Dozens of European colonisers were making a fortune from trading in tobacco, dyes, cotton, sugar, hardwoods and so on.

Then a Clare man named Bernardo O'Brien came to Brazil in 1620. He created a colony called Coconut Grove after bringing a group of workers from Ireland to build a wood and earthen fort on the Amazon. As O'Brien was committed to his life in Brazil and determined to build a good life, he learnt the language of the local Arruan people. His workers also became fluent and their local knowledge became a huge asset and made them expert navigators. With a large number of Irish immigrants, a sizeable Irish community was established. The first St Patrick's Day was celebrated on 17 March in 1770. It was held at a church built by devout Catholic and wealthy farmer Lancelot Belfort (1708-1775) in the state of Maranhão, northern Brazil.

As in numerous other places worldwide, many Irish soldiers became mercenaries serving in the Brazilian Army. Admiral Sir Robert Otway (1770-1846) was a senior Royal Navy officer. Born in the family home of Castle Otway in County Tipperary, he was engaged in various battles and wars. After serving as commander-in-chief after the Napoleonic Wars, he arrived in Brazil. Due to his avid support for Brazil during the Brazilian War of Independence, he was presented with the Order of the Southern Cross when Brazil finally gained independence. Among other notable early Irish soldiers in the Brazilian Army were Diago Nicolau Keating, Diago O'Grady and Jorge Cowan.

During the fight against Argentina of 1825-1828, the Brazilian Emperor Dom Pedro I asked Irish-born Colonel William Cotter in the Brazilian Army to recruit Irish soldiers to form an Irish regiment. He was sent back to County Cork in 1826. He put advertisements in local newspapers and notices at churches in counties

Waterford and Cork. As a result, he returned with between 2,400 and 2,800 mostly illiterate and impoverished rural people who had no knowledge of the military or Brazil. As they were planning to settle down after the war, the newly recruited soldiers brought their wives and children to Rio de Janeiro. Cottar had promised them a military contract that consisted of free passage, pay and allowances equal to 6 shillings per day, food, and a grant of 50 acres of land after five years of service. The offer sounded too good to be true. As it turned out, it was. Cotter's promises were all fabrications and the reality was appallingly harsh. Neglected and disappointed, but unable to return to Ireland, deeply angered men were involved in the Soldier's Revolt in Rio de Janeiro in 1828 when marauding bands of soldiers looted and burnt officers' homes, destroying large parts of the city. After the revolt, some of them moved to other Brazilian provinces, such as Bahia, Santa Catarina and Rio Grande do Sul, or neighbouring countries and earned a living as farmers.

Another failed attempt was made by an Irish Catholic priest, Father T. Donovan. He brought some 400 people from County Wexford in the 1850s to populate the southern provinces without realising the land was too barren for agricultural usage. Consequently, most of them ended up moving to Argentina.

Another colonisation experiment that ended in disaster was when Irish immigrants in New York, including a group of poverty-stricken famine victims, were recruited by Irish priests. The Irish Jesuit Father Joseph Lazenby, along with an Irish Catholic priest, Father George Montgomery, tried to develop Irish Catholic communities in 1868 and recruited more than 300 Irish people. It also sounded promising at first but the area was prone to natural disasters and many of the people who went were killed when there was a flood and those who survived had to move elsewhere.

There were, however, some highly skilled Irish entrepreneurs and professionals who made ordinary immigrants' lives better. William Scully (1819?-1885) was born in Buolick, County Tipperary, into a family of minor Catholic landlords and emigrated to Brazil in the 1850s. He became a meticulous businessman, journalist and the owner/publisher of a weekly newspaper, the Anglo-Brazilian *The Times in Rio de Janeiro*, from 1865 to 1884. The paper included general Brazilian news, political commentaries, commercial reports, market prices, and maritime and immigration news.

Daniel Robert O'Sullivan (1865-1921) was a medical doctor by training and profession, but he established his career as an army officer and diplomat, serving as British consul in Bahia, São Paulo and Rio de Janeiro.

The Irish nationalist Roger Casement (1864-1916) also held high positions for the British Government in Brazil from 1906 to 1911. He first worked as a British consul in Santos, then as consular official in Belém do Pará and finally he became consul-general in Rio de Janeiro. During his stay in Brazil, he produced various writings by experiencing and observing local people and their society, and was knighted for his investigative work on the local Indians. However, because of his cooperation with the German Government during the First World War, when he tried to help in the fight for Irish independence, he was hanged for treason by the British Government in 1916. His knighthood was stripped from him just before his execution.

VENEZUELA

The Liberator, Simón Bolívar (1783-1830), was an eminent political and military leader from Venezuela who played a major role in the fight for Latin American Spanish colonies' independence. Bolívar, who was partial to the Irish, came to London in 1810 as head of a diplomatic mission to recruit soldiers. It is estimated that his army had up to 7,000 Irish soldiers, including veterans of the Napoleonic Wars, who travelled with Bolívar's army all across the South American continent and helped secure independence for Venezuela, Colombia, Ecuador, Peru, Bolivia and Panama. One of the most significant Irish regiments was the 1st Venezuelan Rifles, which fought in the Venezuelan War of Independence between 1811 and 1823.

The most outstanding army officer in the South American wars of independence was William Ferguson (1800-1828). Like other Irish soldiers and officers who were fighting for Bolívar, he travelled to serve in various South American countries such as Venezuela, Columbia, Panama, Ecuador, Peru and Bolivia. Born in Ballinderry, County Antrim, to a family of linen drapers in Belfast, he lived a relatively short life. He was serving as an aide-de-camp to Bolívar in Bogotá, Colombia, when he was killed protecting Bolívar's life in an assassination attempt. He was a Protestant but the Colombian Government gave him a public funeral, burying his remains in the national cathedral and erecting a grand monument in his honour.

Another distinguished soldier was Thomas Charles Wright (1799-1868) who was born in Drogheda, County Louth. Like many Irish men at that time, he went to the naval college at Portsmouth and joined HMS *Newcastle*, a Royal Navy ship. He eventually became an officer in Bolívar's British Legion in 1817 and served in various South and Central American countries, such as Venezuela, Ecuador and Panama. After being sent to Guayaquil in Ecuador, he developed a naval force in order to patrol the area. He is known as a founder of the Ecuadorian naval school.

Wexford man John Devereux (1778-1854) was a principal army recruiter for the Irish Legion in Bolívar's army. After migrating to the US, he became involved in military activities. He recruited 5,000 men and raised an Irish Legion by claiming that he was a general in the Irish Army who had led the Irish Catholics in the fight for emancipation. He had been promised 175 dollars per soldier sent to Venezuela, which was a substantial amount of money in those days. Although Bolívar's soldiers were not paid, Devereux deceived future volunteers by saying they would receive much more than in the British Army, as well as land grants when their term of service ended.

Back in Dublin, Devereux organised an event called the Irish Friends of South American Independence. With Daniel O'Connell's support, alluring posters and handbills, many young people were attracted to join the cause. Inspired by his father's friendship, Morgan O'Connell, Daniel's second son, became an officer and an enlisted military aid for Bolívar. As the Irish Legion's youngest officer, he landed on Venezuela's Margarita Island in 1820. Generally, Irish soldiers didn't know anything about tropical climates, dysentery, typhus, yellow fever, fleas, mosquitoes, strange food, humidity, impure water and all the other nasty things that accompany hot climates. After arriving on Margarita Island, off the coast of Venezuela, many struggled just to survive. General Mariano Montilla took command of the Irish Legion but spoke almost no English. Without clear objectives or specific directions, the number of Irish soldiers instantly decreased by half – approximately 1,000 died or deserted. Some of those who remained were living with serious mental and physical problems such as alcoholism. As discipline and motivation had disappeared, the force was disarmed and shipped to the British colony of Jamaica. Some ended up joining the British Army there while others who could afford the passage settled in Canada. Devereux was eventually arrested and imprisoned. After he was released, he spent the rest of his life in the US. He lived a relatively long life on a Venezuelan pension.

Among qualified high-ranking officers recruited by Devereux, there was a Cork man, Francis Burdett O'Connor (1791-1871), who came to Margarita Island. He served as an officer in the Irish Legion in Venezuela and later became minister of war in Bolivia. His uncle, Arthur O'Connor, also fought in France for Robert Emmet's rebellion of the United Irishmen. After the liberation of Colombia, he and his regiment of approximately 170 soldiers joined the United Army of Liberation in Peru in 1824. General Antonio José de Sucre asked him to command the Campaign in Upper Peru, and he was later appointed military governor of Tarija, in current Bolivia. He issued a proclamation in 1827 asking Irish people to populate the 'New Erin' of Tarija. His last days were spent in Tarija, farming and writing about his front-line experiences and his life.

COLOMBIA

It is estimated that up to 2,000 Irish soldiers were led by Irish officers in the Irish Legion of Simón Bolívar's army in Colombia and fought for the Colombian War of Independence. One of the most prominent commanders was Dubliner James Rooke (1770-1819), who first served for the British Army and then joined Bolívar's army. As commander under Bolívar, Rooke led the Irish troops, which did extremely well during the Vargas Swamp Battle as well as the Battle of Boyacá. He died near Tunja, Colombia, shortly after losing his arm.

Much of our knowledge of Irish soldiers' contribution to Bolívar's cause comes from Cork man Daniel Florence O'Leary (1802-1854). He was a military general and aide-de-camp under Bolívar. O'Leary knew he was experiencing history in the making and when Bolívar died in 1830, he kept all his closest confidant's war documents, despite the order to destroy them. He appreciated the great value of Bolívar's personal documents, so he spent the rest of his life sorting through them as well as writing his own first-hand account of the revolutionary battles he fought with Bolívar. After O'Leary's death, his son, Simón Bolívar O'Leary, published his father's detailed memoirs. Not only was this valuable for the front-line military accounts of the glorious battles but it also analysed how the struggle for independence in South America corresponded with the Irish struggle for independence. During this period, the Irish political leader and liberator Daniel O'Connell (1775-1847) and Bolívar were exchanging ideas by letters. Although both of them were called the Liberator, they were two completely different people – Bolívar believed force was necessary to achieve freedom while O'Connell preferred non-violent democratic activism. Thanks to his meticulous and compelling way of telling stories, O'Leary earned one of the highest honours in Latin American history; O'Leary died in Bogotá, Colombia but he was later laid to rest in the National Pantheon of Venezuela, the same sacred burial place of Bolívar.

Like O'Leary, Arthur Sandes (1793-1832) also became an inspirational military figure. He worked as an officer under Bolívar and became one of his closest allies. Born in County Kerry, he was recruited in London and came to Venezuela as commander of the Regiment of Rifles. When Irish Commander Robert Pigott in Angostura, Colombia, left the regiment due to ill health, Sandes succeeded him and stayed there for the rest of the war. After serving with distinction in various regions, such as Peru and Ecuador, he became governor of Azuay and spent the rest of his life in Cuenca, Ecuador, where he is considered a great Ecuadorean hero.

Other high-ranking officers from Ireland in Bolívar's army include Kildare man William Aylmer (1778-1820), Cork man Francisco Burdett O'Connor (1791-1871) and Dubliner James Towers English (1782-1819).

Irish medical doctors – often with Trinity College degrees – were also actively involved in the wars of independence, travelling with the navy and army, providing medical services to the soldiers. After moving to Colombia, Dr Hugo Blair Brown (1787-1864) spent his entire life looking after the sick and wounded. Originally from a Protestant background, he converted to Catholicism in Medellín, where he married a local woman.

Since the Legion of Mary was established by Frank Duff in Dublin in 1921, the Irish Catholic lay people have been active all across the world. After spending some time with the Irish Christian Brothers, Alfie Lambe (1932-1959) from Tullamore, County Offaly, joined the Legion of Mary. He and Seamus Grace were sent to Bogotá in 1953 in order to establish a Legion praesidium, or branch. They later expanded their mission not only in Colombia but all across South American countries, especially in Argentina, Ecuador, Uruguay and Brazil. Lambe was very good at languages and he quickly became fluent in Spanish and Portuguese, which allowed him to train countless locals. He died in Buenos Aires and is buried in the vault of the Irish Christian Brothers in the Recoleta Cemetery.

URUGUAY

As part of the Spanish Empire, Uruguay, known as Banda Oriental until the 1900s, fought against Spain, Portugal and Britain before finally becoming independent in 1828. Irish settlers started arriving from the 1700s onwards and many of these men were caught up in bloody battles during this chaotic time. It is estimated there are more than 100,000 Uruguayans who are of Irish descents, principally in the capital city, Montevideo.

Irish captain in the British Army, John McNamara, failed to occupy Colonia del Sacramento in 1762, but Brigadier-General Samuel Auchmuty of the British Army successfully occupied Montevideo in 1807. During this short period of British rule, which lasted only fourteen months, a considerable number of Irish and British people, many of them merchants, arrived in Uruguay and settled there.

One of the most famous Irish men to have gone to Uruguay is Peter Campbell (1780-1832), or Pedro Campbell, the father of Uruguayan Navy. Born in County Tipperary, he first enlisted with the British Army and came to South America to join the British invasions of the Río de la Plata under Anglo-Irish general William Carr Beresford, the illegitimate son of the 1st Marquess of Waterford. Britain lost but Campbell stayed in the region with some fellow soldiers. With his great military skill, Campbell eventually became a guerrilla leader who fought against the Spanish Army and served under the father of Uruguayan nationhood, José Gervasio Artigas (1764-1850) who is one of the country's most significant national heroes. Campbell played a key role in the Corrientes province – the present-day north-east Argentina, which is surrounded by Uruguay, Paraguay and Brazil. He trained and hired many local soldiers and established a regiment composed mostly of indigenous people. With his great leadership ability, he took charge of, and successfully led, the Uruguayan naval forces. As a result, Artigas appointed him the first naval commander-in-chief and he eventually established the Uruguayan Navy.

In 1836, thousands of Irish people, especially from Kilrane parish in County Wexford, came to work as sheep farmers and settled in the Rio Negro district, while others from counties Westmeath and Longford moved to the Pysandú area. This led to a boom in wool production and its export became key to the country's economy. A large demand from the expanding textile industry in Europe meant the Argentinian economy grew rapidly and became part of the world economy. As a consequence, wool prices increased. Uruguay was a popular destination until about the mid-nineteenth century. These settlers included a substantial number of famine immigrants who arrived via the US.

Owning land meant a lot to Catholic Irish people as they couldn't own land back in Ireland. Some high-profile Irish landowners in Uruguay included James Gaynor (1802-1892), John Maguire (18?-1905) and Laois man William Lawlor (1822-1909). They owned substantial property on both sides of the Argentine-Uruguayan border, as many ranchers did in those days. Among wealthy rural settlers were J. Hughes in Paysandú and foreman Robert Young. Young had 10 square leagues of land in Estancia Bichadero, planted tropical trees in the pampas and owned approximately 100,000 sheep and cattle by 1875. The people who worked for him were all from Ireland. With his successful business, he established a city called Young in Rio Negro.

Christian missionaries, educators and doctors were ubiquitous in Uruguay. There were also a few Irish and/or Catholic institutions, such as the Irish Christian Brothers School and the Stella Maris School, which was established by Patrick C. Kelly in 1955. Alfie Lambe of the Legion of Mary also established a branch in Montevideo in 1956. Irish physician Constantine Conyngham O'Connor (1807-1868) was recognised and greatly respected by the local government for his efficient work during the epidemic in Montevideo in 1856. A Dublin-born surgeon-general, Louis Arthur de Fleury (1842-1897), who worked in the Charity Hospital was also well recognised in Uruguay.

PARAGUAY

Paraguay was a part of the Argentine provinces under the Spanish Empire. As a landlocked country, it was used as a battleground and saw its fair share of political turmoil until it became independent in 1811.

A Jesuit from Limerick, Thomas Field (1547-1626), was one of the first Irish people to move to Paraguay. After spending more than ten years in Brazil, he came to Paraguay in 1587 and spent his whole life on Jesuit missions in Asunción. He was a pioneering missionary who paved the way for other Jesuits to spread mission activities in South America. Some distinguished missionaries who followed in his footsteps were Father Thomas Browne (1656-1717) from County Waterford and Brother William Leny (1692-1760) from County Dublin. The missions thrived initially and were involved in various cultural activities such as printing publications in the local Guaraní language by using their own early printing press. However, the Jesuits were eventually all expelled by the Spanish Government as part of reforms to their administration system.

The Gills were one of the oldest Irish-Paraguayan families. It is believed that many people in Paraguay with this surname are descended from Thomas Gill who arrived in Asunción in 1730. Among the many notable people who have carried the name, the most famous one is Juan B. Gill (1840-1877), who was president of Paraguay. There were many other Irish immigrants who became accomplished leaders and prominent founding fathers. Carlos Morphi, or Carlos Murphy, founded the cities of Caacupé in 1770 and Lambaré in 1766. Descended from a Cork family, he served as Lieutenant Colonel of Spain and governor of Paraguay between 1766 and 1772.

The most powerful woman in the history of Paraguay is undoubtedly Eliza Alicia Lynch (1835-1886). She was born in Charleville, County Cork, and migrated to Paris with her family during the famine. After establishing herself as a courtesan, which was not uncommon for beautiful young girls in those days, she met Francisco Solano López (1826-1870) in Paris in 1853. He was training in the Napoleonic Army. López's father was Carlos Antonio López, president of Paraguay, which was one of the richest nations in South America at the time. They fell in love and he brought his pregnant mistress back home to Paraguay. Although they were never married, she bore a total of six children with him. He soon became president and dictator in Paraguay and Lynch became the most prominent female figure of the nation. When she was in power, she caused controversy. She is believed to be responsible for provoking her partner to start the Paraguayan War, also known as the Triple Alliance War (1864-1870). During the war, Lynch organised a group of soldiers' wives, daughters and other female family members to help support the soldiers. With her power and unlimited resources during these chaotic times, she started building all kinds of extravagant things, such as palaces and opera houses, and purchasing fine jewels and vast swathes land at low prices. All the money she made ended up back in France where she spent the last years of her life. She certainly was part of the bloody history of Paraguay, but she is now considered a national heroine.

PUERTO RICO

Although not geographically located in South America, the Irish experience in Spanish Colonial Puerto Rico is similar to that of the Irish in South America. As Roman Catholic Spain encouraged non-Spanish Catholics to populate their colonies, such as Puerto Rico and Cuba, Irish famine victims emigrated en masse to Puerto Rico via the US and contributed to the country's education, politics and economy, notably the sugar industry. The majority of Irish immigrants in Puerto Rico intermarried with local and other non-Irish people, adopted the local language and integrated well.

The first Irishmen poured into Puerto Rico as Wild Geese (see 'France', p. 163) during the sixteenth century. During this time, an intense power struggle took place over control of the Caribbean by major European armies. These first migrants were followed by Irish soldiers who arrived with the English Army in 1585. When they left or finished their duties, they joined the Spanish Army and remained there after their service had finished. As the route was already established, waves of Irish people followed them to Puerto Rico.

Among Puerto Rico's outstanding military figures was Field Marshal Alejandro O'Reilly (1723-1794), who was born in Baltrasna, County Meath. He was an inspector-general of infantry for Spain and became known as the father of the Puerto Rican Militia. Trained as a military engineer, Galway man Colonel Tomás O'Daly (1700?-1781) worked as a chief engineer in San Juan, the capital of Puerto Rico, upon arrival. Thanks to his work modernising the defences of San Juan, he received land and developed it into a sugar hacienda which he named the Hacienda San Patricio, after the Irish patron saint, St Patrick. Many Irish people followed in O'Daly's footsteps by owning sugar and tobacco plantations and running businesses to develop the country's fledgling economy. Irish brothers Robert and Josiah Archbald brought the first steam-operated mill in Puerto Rico in 1823 to help increase sugar production.

6

AUSTRALIA AND
NEW ZEALAND

AUSTRALIA

At school, we all learn about Australia as a country of convicts, or a penal colony. When the British took control of the region, they originally thought of using it as a dumping ground for prisoners and other unwanted people – as they had done in some regions of the Americas. Many Irish convicts were sent to Australia. At the same time, a considerable number of involuntary and voluntary migrants also travelled to the region. Consequently, one third of the Australian population was Irish by the late nineteenth century. In terms of numbers, more Irish people went to the US but in terms of a proportion, a much higher percentage of Australia's population was Irish.

It is estimated up to 30 per cent of the current population of Australia have some degree of Irish ancestry. The majority were Catholic but about 20 per cent of the Irish immigrants to Australia were Protestant. Merchants, soldiers, gold miners, the religiously oppressed, would-be farmers and settlers from all walks of life came to Australia of their own free will with dreams and aspirations. And, of course, as was the case in the Americas, indigenous people had been living there long before the first European discovered Australia. While the early settlers mistreated the indigenous Aborigines, some

Irish were known to have got on well with them and there are even a few aboriginal Australians of Irish descent.

Convicts

Although the transportation of convicts to Australia may have been occurring from an earlier date, it wasn't until after the American War of Independence (1775-1783) that Australia became the primary penal colony of the British Empire. The journey from England to Australia took nearly eight months and sometimes longer if the weather was bad. Although estimates differ, it is thought up to 50,000 so-called convicts were shipped from Ireland to Australia via the UK from 1787 to 1868, when the system officially ended. A minimum sentence of seven years was most common for those convicted, but they could be sentenced to ten years, fourteen years, or even penal servitude for life.

Many Irish convicts were political prisoners who were involved in the Irish Rebellion of 1798, Robert Emmet's 1803 Rising and the Young Irelander Rebellion of 1848. Some of the political prisoners sent to Australia after the Irish Rebellion of 1798 were priests – including Father James Dixon from Wexford, Father Peter O'Neil from Youghal and Father James Harold from Dublin– who were sent there because of their alleged complicity. Dozens of young children who stole food out of hunger were also shipped there. Male convicts habitually took their wives and children with them to Australia in the 1840s. Convicts were able to officially apply to travel with their families or for them to come out later at the expense of the British Government. Between 1828 and 1848, the government gave financial assistance to the relatives of convicts who were shipped to Australia in order to help them settle there.

The mainland of Australia was divided into five political regions: New South Wales, Western Australia, Victoria, South Australia and Queensland, as well as two insular colonies, Tasmania, and New Zealand, or Great Britain of the South. The penal settlements where Irish people were principally sent to included New South Wales (penal colony period 1788-1842), Victoria (1803-1849), Tasmania, previously called Van Dieman's Land (1812-1853), Queensland (1823-1850) and Western Australia (1850-1868).

Convicts were customarily sent from their local gaol but in order to ship a horde of people in a systematic fashion, holding prisons called depots were set up in the early 1800s. A couple of depots were provided in counties Cork and Dublin, and there was even one especially for women. After the Great Famine, a depot in Smithfield, County Dublin, and one on Spike Island in County Cork were briefly used. Doctors were scared of epidemics and examined convicts thoroughly in the depot to ensure they didn't have diseases such as dysentery, typhus or cholera. The people who went to Australia were generally treated much better than those who left for America as they needed to be healthy and fit to build the colony. Unlike the people who travelled on coffin ships, there were physicians on board to look after the convicts. Equipped with nutritious food, clean clothes and hygienic berths, they were treated as humanely as possible, both physically and mentally. As a result, they became the great labour force that developed the colony for nearly 100 years during the transportation period.

To prove the point, an English judge and royal commissioner, John Thomas Bigge (1780-1843), visited Australia and wrote a report on the transportation system. He noted:

> The convicts embarked in Ireland generally arrive in New South Wales in a very healthy state, and are found to be more obedient and more sensible of kind treatment during the passage than any other class. Their separation from their native country is observed to make a stronger impression upon their minds, both on their departure and during the voyage.

The first group of convicts was officially shipped from Portsmouth to Botany Bay, New South Wales, and arrived in 1788. The eighth governor and the first Irish representative of the new settlement in New South Wales was Major-General Sir Richard Bourke (1778-1855). Born in Dublin and educated at Oxford, he joined the British Army and served in Uruguay, Malta and South Africa. With ample international experience, he came to Australia and effectively served as governor of New South Wales between 1831 and 1837. During his tenure, he contributed to the local economy, which rapidly flourished through land management, the emancipation of convicts and the cessation of the transportation of convicts.

Van Diemen's Land, which was renamed Tasmania in 1856, is an island of about the size of Ireland near the south of Victoria. Colonel David Collins (1756-1810) was the first lieutenant governor of the colony. Born in London to an Irish father from County Offaly, he was placed in command to establish a penal colony on the island when the first group of hundreds of convicts were shipped.

Although many of them were treated reasonably, the lives of convicts were far from good. Some of them worked for eighteen hours a day and lived in a stifling environment. Countless prisoners tried to escape throughout the period of transportation. When they were caught, they often received severe punishments such as flogging or, in some cases, hanging. During the early period, a substantial number of convicts were native Irish speakers who were mainly Fenian prisoners. Some of the other convicts were annoyed by their foreign language and Gaelic speakers were often the targets of bullying and harassment – in severe cases, they were tortured when they spoke Gaelic.

One notable convict sent to Australia was Michael Dwyer (1772-1825) from County Wicklow. As a United Irishmen leader in the 1798 Rebellion, he fought a guerrilla campaign against the British Army in the Wicklow Mountains. He was captured and transported to New South Wales in 1805 with his wife. After finishing his sentence, he acquired a nearby farm and became actively involved in the local Catholic community by helping to build St Mary's church. He eventually became chief constable of Liverpool in New South Wales but he was removed from this position in 1820 as he had developed a drink problem.

Joseph Holt (1756-1826) from County Wicklow also fought in the Wicklow Mountains as a United Irish general and was exiled to Australia. He sailed with his wife and son from County Cork and arrived in Sydney in 1800. There, he worked as a farm manager. He eventually came back to Ireland, where he died.

John Mitchel (1815-1875), from County Derry, was a solicitor by profession and an assistant editor of *The Nation* in Dublin under Charles Gavan Duffy, the Irish journalist who later became a politician in Australia. Mitchel launched a weekly newspaper called the *United Irishman*, which reflected the militant views of the Young

Ireland Movement. He was charged with sedition and sent to the Caribbean first, then Van Diemen's Land. As an observant journalist, he didn't waste his time while serving his sentence. He took notes on his experience and wrote a book called *Jail Journal*. Although it was a tough time for him, he described the enchanting scenery of Tasmania, the isle of beauty. This was the place where the most prominent leaders of the Young Irelanders were sent. Among them were William Smith O'Brien, Thomas Francis Meagher, Terence Bellew McManus, Patrick O'Donoghue, John Martin and Kevin Izod O'Doherty.

Another high-profile convict who utilised his skills and expertise in the fledgling nation was Edward O'Shaughnessy (1801-1840). He was convicted of collecting taxes under false pretences and sent to Australia. A graduate of Trinity College, his intelligence and wide knowledge of literature gave him the opportunity to work as editor, journalist and poet for the official journal of the colony, the *Sydney Gazette*.

The most internationally famous Irish-Australian is probably Ned Kelly. Depending on your perspective, he was an infamous outlaw or an Irish-Australian version of Robin Hood. Edward 'Ned' Kelly (1854-1880) was born in Beveridge, Victoria. His father was an Irish convict from County Tipperary who was sent to Tasmania for stealing pigs. After finishing his sentence, he moved to Port Phillip in Victoria and started a family. Ned grew up to become a bushranger but had extremely troubled teenage years. As a youngster, Ned was arrested a couple of times for stealing, alleged assault and being a suspected accomplice – but then he formed the Kelly gang and his crimes became more serious. The police force in those days was dominated by the Irish, especially in Victoria, where more than 80 per cent of police were Irish-born and the Kelly gang killed three Irish police officers in 1878. The gang became the most wanted outlaws in Victoria. Ned, famously clad in armour, fought several gun battles with the police, but eventually he was arrested. He was tried before the Irish judge Redmond Barry, found guilty and hanged at the Melbourne Jail. As he died young, he became the symbol of Irish Australian resistance – a legend.

Assisted immigration

For those who wanted to settle in Australia but who could not afford passage fees, there were various assisted emigrant schemes, both public and private. The schemes, which paid some or all of the costs, started in the early 1800s and were extremely helpful for those willing to start a new life but who had no means to leave. Throughout the century, principally after the Great Famine years, Irish people streamed out of their homeland in search of a better life.

County Donegal was one of the most impoverished counties and the Donegal Relief Fund was created for those people who were in need of financial help. The fund paid a depositor, or sponsor, which was a portion of the assisted passage required by the New South Wales immigration deposit regulations. The depositor then paid 4 pounds to ship someone from Ireland and the government paid the rest of the passage money. By the late nineteenth century, hundreds of thousands of Irish were arriving in Sydney as a result of having been sponsored under these schemes. Free passage was targeted at single women willing to emigrate and there were many posters and advertisements for the schemes in Ireland.

The first bishop of Brisbane, James Quinn, is known to have brought a large number of Irish people to Queensland through the assisted scheme. As the region filled up with Irish settlers thanks to him, it was called Quinnsland, according to a popular quip of the day.

The peak year for Irish immigration was 1891. The census from that year shows that nearly 30 per cent of immigrants were from the British Isles. The numbers subsequently fell but nothing stopped the influx of people arriving in the region. When the southern part of Ireland became the Republic after the Second World War, the residents there stopped being British subjects and couldn't benefit the assisted passage but Northern Irish people were still eligible and continued to use the scheme.

Orphans

The Australian population became predominantly male. To remedy this imbalance, more than 4,000 orphan girls between the ages of 14 and 20 were shipped to Australia during the famine period. Two girls out of every three brought by the emigrant ships were Irish. Most of them worked as domestic servants and married the young men in the colony. Some of the more unfortunate girls were abused and treated badly by their employers. Without adequate care and support, or the means to earn their own living, some of them eventually ran away and became prostitutes. It is believed the majority of those girls died young in atrocious conditions.

A plethora of agencies of the Catholic Church in Ireland, such as the Sisters of Mercy, played a big part in this child migration scheme shipping orphans abroad. The Sisters of Mercy first came to Perth, Western Australia, in 1846. As they were the first religious order to help settlers and newcomers in Australia, they had a visible presence and built a substantial number of institutions, schools, orphanages and churches over the years. In 1888, a couple of Irish nuns from the Sisters of Charity came to Parramatta, New South Wales, when there was a large influx of Irish newcomers. They built twenty-four primary schools, five secondary schools and two orphanages.

A substantial number of male orphans were also sent to Australia by the Christian Brothers. In 1938, Brother Louis Conlon, who was the head of the Christian Brothers in Australia, took part in a campaign to increase the number of children being sent to Catholic institutions in Australia. The Church had absolute power and authority back home and although there were some who took advantage of this, there were also many genuine people devoted to helping forced Irish immigrants spiritually and emotionally.

Local Irish communities generally supported the growth of the Catholic Church. One of the priests who laid the foundation for the Catholic community in Australia was Father John McEncroe (1794-1868), a native of Rathsalla, near Cashel in Tipperary. After entering the seminary of Maynooth, he became an ordained priest. During his early years as a priest, he was involved in missionary work under Cork man Bishop John England in the US, an experience which opened his eyes. McEncroe was deeply inspired by American democracy and he also learned the power of the media while in America. He became editor of Bishop England's *United States Catholic Miscellany* and he believed it was necessary to have a Catholic press. He returned to Ireland but emigrated to Sydney before long and established the *Sydney Freeman's Journal*, which was a high-class literary weekly newspaper. He looked after convicts and played a crucial role as part of the leading charitable institutions in Sydney. As a member of benevolent societies and a pioneer of the temperance movement, he dedicated his life to Catholic education. He introduced the Sisters of Mercy and the Marist Brothers into his parish schools. He died at St Patrick's Church Hill where he had been parish priest since 1861.

Another notable Roman Catholic bishop was Patrick Bonaventure Geoghegan (1805-1864). As an orphan himself, he had a tough childhood growing up in Dublin. His relations initially wanted to put him into a Protestant institution but a Franciscan priest helped them place him in a Catholic orphanage. He grew up to be a Franciscan priest and was later appointed to establish the first Catholic mission in Melbourne. To cater for a substantial number of newly arrived Irish Catholic immigrants living in the area, he built schools, churches and laid the foundation of St Francis's church, which was opened in 1845. Geoghegan came back to Ireland to recruit priests for the mission in Australia. When Dr Francis Murphy passed away in 1858, he was appointed bishop of Adelaide, South Australia. As a founding member of the local Catholic community, he established many schools and twenty churches, as well as the chancel and side altars of St Francis Xavier's Cathedral.

Politicians

As in other countries where the Irish settled in significant numbers, graduates from Irish colleges, especially Trinity College, were significant in the development of Australia. Their expertise was a great asset in all core fields – politics, law, medicine and media. As principle founding members of Australia, the Irish were politically active from the earliest days of the parliamentary government there. For instance, the Legislative Assembly's early speakers in Victoria were all Irish.

Cork man Sir Francis Murphy (1809-1891) was educated at medical institutions in Cork, Trinity College and London. He came to Sydney in 1836 when Governor Richard Bourke appointed him colonial surgeon. After abandoning his medical career, he became a politician and farmer. He was the first speaker of the Legislative Assembly, holding the seat of Murray Boroughs.

Sir Redmond Barry (1813-1880) was a colonial judge in Victoria who played an important role in Australian society. A Cork man with a degree from Trinity College, he was called to the bar in Dublin. He went to Sydney to work in 1837 and he eventually became commissioner of the Court of Requests. He then worked as the first solicitor-general of Victoria, before becoming a judge of the Supreme Court of Victoria. His was hugely influential in the development of the Australian legal system. He was also involved in the foundation of the Royal Melbourne Hospital, the University of Melbourne, the State Library of Victoria, the Supreme Court Library in Melbourne, the Melbourne Public Library and the Sunbury Industrial School.

Another Trinity College graduate, Moses Wilson Gray (1813-1875) was born in Claremorris, County Mayo. He was admitted both to the Irish Bar and the US Bar. He published a booklet, *Self-paying Colonization*, in North America after travelling in the US and Canada, and researching the colonisation of impoverished Irish tenants. He moved back home and worked as editor of the *Freeman's Journal*, the oldest nationalistic newspaper. In 1856, he emigrated to Melbourne with his friend Charles Gavan Duffy. Although he was admitted to the Victorian Bar, with his passion for writing, he became a law reporter. He was involved in the United Australian Society and the Eight Hours Labour League. He moved to New Zealand in 1862 and became district judge in the Otago region.

One of the most influential politicians was Sir Charles Gavan Duffy (1816-1903). Born in County Monaghan, he first worked as a journalist in Dublin. As a passionate Irish nationalist, he wrote with the desire to be a catalyst for nationalist feeling. After emigrating with his family to Australia in 1856, he settled in Victoria. He became deputy for Tipperary-born John O'Shanassy who was the second premier in Victoria. Duffy served as commissioner for public works, president of the Board of Land and Works and commissioner for Crown Lands and Survey during the period when there were not many Irish Catholics serving as cabinet ministers. He eventually became premier and chief secretary and his sons also followed in his footsteps. John Gavan Duffy was a politician from 1874 to 1904 and another son, Sir Frank Gavan Duffy, became chief justice of the High Court of Australia between 1931 and 1935.

Versatile politician and businessman, Sir John O'Shanassy (1818-1883) from Ballinahow, County Tipperary, first came to Sydney to join his relative. He started his political career after winning a by-election to become a member of the Melbourne Council in 1846. He was elected prime minister of Victoria three times and served for more than thirty years, making him a commanding figure in Victorian public life. The leading lay Catholic O'Shanassy focused on improving the education system for Catholic Irish immigrants. He had a lifelong friendship with Father Patrick Bonaventure Geoghegan. As a shrewd businessman, he played a key role as chairman of the Colonial Bank, also known as the Diggers Bank, as well as being a founder and president of St Patrick's Society.

Mary Lee (1821-1909), *neé* Walsh, was a suffragist who changed the course of labour history. She was a social reformer who campaigned for the women's right to vote. Born in County Monaghan, she initially moved to Adelaide to look after her son who was ill. After he died, she remained in Australia as she couldn't afford a return ticket. With her qualities of leadership and perseverance, she dedicated her life to achieving social and political reform. In 1894, women in South Australia were the first in Australia to gain the parliamentary vote. Although she struggled financially in the last part of her life, she continued to help women with their suffrage campaigns in other states.

A talented businessman, politician and Catholic community leader Michael O'Grady (1824-1876) came from Frenchpark, County Roscommon. He initially moved to London to work and met Charles Gavan Duffy there. They had a long friendship that lasted even after emigrating to Australia. He was sent to Melbourne to open a branch office of the insurance company he had been working for. He soon became a representative of Villiers and Heytesbury and also worked for the Irish Catholic community in Victoria by improving education and people's daily lives. As an avid supporter of Catholic charities, he became one of the founders of the weekly Catholic paper, the *Advocate*. For his contribution to the Catholic community, he was made a Knight of St Gregory by Pope Pius IX in 1871.

Thomas Henry Fitzgerald (1824-1888) was born in Carrick-macross, County Monaghan. After qualifying as an engineer, he moved to New Zealand where his brother had already settled. Fitzgerald worked at a number of jobs, including surveyor, a super-intendent, an agent for a shipping company, a politician and colonial treasurer. Like many other Irish immigrants who left home, he then became a pioneer sugar cane farmer in Queensland in Australia. Taking advantage of Brisbane's sub-tropical climate, he established a couple of sugar plantations. Adventurous and skilful, Fitzgerald started applying a new method and as a result sugar cultivation vastly increased, which created employment for others. With his pioneer-ing spirit, he was ambitious and wanted to develop a settlement. He established the town of Innisfail in the north of Queensland in 1880 with the help of the Brisbane Convent of Mercy. His offspring went on to be prominent and widely involved in local businesses, law and politics, like himself.

Born in Omagh, County Tyrone, Sir Charles MacMahon (1824-1891) first served in Canada as an ensign with the British Army. He came to Melbourne in 1852 and joined the local police force. After helping to abolish magistrates' control over police, he became a poli-tician representing West Melbourne. Ambrose Henry Spencer Kyte (1822-1868) was from Nenagh, County Tipperary. He was a politi-cian, merchant and property investor. After arriving in Melbourne in 1840 and working as a brewer's labourer, he became a member of the Lower House and protectionist politician.

Dubliner Sir Bryan O'Loghlen (1828-1905) made an inspirational contribution to Irish immigrants in Australia and democratic institu-tions. He paved the way for all Irish people as premier of Victoria and Attorney General and treasurer. After studying at Trinity College Dublin and Oscott College, Birmingham, England, he was admit-ted to the Irish Bar. Just like many politically motivated youngsters in those days, he joined the Young Ireland movement. After arriv-ing in Melbourne in 1862, he was immediately appointed a crown prosecutor. Between 1863 and 1877, he was known as the most industrious and successful crown prosecutor for the Melbourne dis-trict. He was elected to the Victorian Legislative Assembly for West Melbourne and became a liberal politician in Victoria. In order to provide land for farmers, he played a huge role in ending the power of the landowner-dominated Victorian Legislative Council where there was a dominant British Protestant population as well as tens of thousands of Irish Protestants. As a loyal Catholic and a staunch supporter of the Irish nationalist cause, his life was spent improving the lives of workers and the unemployed.

Galway man Nicholas Fitzgerald (1829-1908) studied at Trinity College and came to Melbourne in 1859 to join his brother who had started the Castlemaine brewery. He was a member of the National Australasian Convention in Sydney. As a Catholic layman, he was awarded the papal knighthood of St Gregory by Pope Leo XIII. He is known as one of the foremost Irish orators of Australia. For more than twenty years, he was an active and leading member of the Legislative Council of Victoria. His debating ability was ranked as first class, which contributed greatly to the promotion of legislation for Catholics. He often spoke at public gatherings for the Church and was involved in the completion St Patrick's Cathedral. In 1863, he married the eldest daughter of John O'Shanassy, Marianne, and they had seven children.

Orange Order

The first Orange Lodge was established in Victoria in 1843. By 1848, there were nine lodges in Sydney with a total of 5,000 Orangemen and by 1900 there were more than 160 branches in Victoria. Women were allowed to join in 1903 and before long, there were nearly 20,000 Orangemen intensely involved with Protestant activities in New South Wales.

Orangemen and Irish Catholic were always getting involved in scuffles with one another. In 1867, a Protestant hall in Melbourne was stoned by Catholic Irish Australians and in retaliation Orangemen shot an 11-year-old Catholic boy dead. Tensions between them again increased when Irish Catholic Henry James O'Farrell attempted to assassinate the Duke of Edinburgh at a Sydney meeting in 1868.

The first lodge was formed in Western Australia in 1886, but as was the case in Canada, Orangeism didn't take root in Australia as well as it did in the US.

Irish soldiers

Ever since the Royal Marines arrived in 1788, the Irish have been an essential part of the armed forces in Australia. Throughout the military history of Australia, a horde of Irish regiments were set up, such as the New South Wales Irish Rifles, the Royal Irish Fusiliers, the Royal Irish Rangers, and so on. During the First World War, the Australian and New Zealand Army Corps (ANZAC) was established as a First World War Army Corps and it included nearly 7,000 Irish men and women. Some of them also served in the Australian Imperial Force and the 1st New Zealand Expeditionary Force. The Australian Army Nursing Service also included a large number of nurses who bore Irish surnames.

Although mechanical engineer Louis Brennan (1852-1932) was not a soldier, he is responsible for some indispensable inventions that were used during conflicts. Born in Castlebar, County Mayo, after emigrating to Melbourne, he developed a torpedo for coastal defence and later patented it in England. He also invented a monorail locomotive with gyroscopic stabilisers and a helicopter.

Sports

Although it is debatable, there is a theory that Australian Rules football is based on Gaelic football. Australian Rules football was being played in Victoria in the early 1840s. Some historians are therefore convinced that Australian football has nothing to do with Gaelic football, arguing that it has been played for longer than Gaelic football. Another theory suggests that it could be the other way round – that Gaelic football could be based on Australian football. One of the founders of the Gaelic Athletic Association (GAA), Archbishop Thomas Croke (1824-1902), who was the bishop of Auckland, New Zealand between 1870 and 1874, could have introduced it to Ireland when he returned home. But the fact is that Irish people had been playing Gaelic football long before the official formation of the GAA – both at home and abroad. They certainly didn't start playing because the GAA was set up. So there is no conclusive evidence indicating who influenced who, but it may be that they have similar origins.

Australian Rules football was refined and firmly established during the Gold Rush in Australia when there were many immigrants from all walks of life in Australia. It probably evolved thanks to the contribution of many different immigrants from different parts of the world who played and altered an Australian Aboriginal game. Irish immigrants certainly contributed their fair share to this local football.

Gold Rush

Irish people flocked to gold fields whenever they heard a rumour of gold being found. The Irish in Australia rushed to California when gold was found there and, likewise, the Irish in California hurried to reach Australia as soon as there was news of gold being struck there.

James William Esmond (1822-1890), from County Wexford, was an agile man. He emigrated to Port Phillip in Victoria and worked at odd jobs, such as driving the mail coach and working at stations, before joining the California gold rush. An intelligent youngster who happened to notice the similarity in the geological formations of the two countries, he tried his luck back in Australia, believing that gold should be abundant. His hunch was right – he became one of the first people to find gold in Australia after making his fortune in the mining town of Clunes, Victoria, in 1851.

Paddy Hannan (1840-1925) from Quin, County Clare, along with Thomas Flanagan and Daniel Shea, found gold near Kalgoorlie, now known as Hannan, in Western Australia in 1893. The Gold Rush in Ballarat in Victoria began in 1851 after Irish immigrants John Dunlop and James Regan discovered gold at Poverty Point. Consequently, approximately 20,000 gold seekers, including a substantial number of Irish immigrants already in Australia, flocked to the Yarrowee Valley, also known as the Ballarat diggings. The population explosion led to the creation and development of a new city.

Life in the goldfields was rough, unfair and lawless. One of the major rebellions that took place was the Eureka Rebellion, which was an uprising of gold miners in Ballarat against the colonial authority of Australia in 1854. Gold miners were hugely dissatisfied with the licence system and local police brutality. It was an Irishman, Peter Fintan Lalor (1827-1889), who led the rebellion. Born in County Laois, he was educated as a civil engineer at Trinity College.

While three of his brothers emigrated to America, Peter and his brother Richard moved to Victoria. He joined the Victorian Gold Rush and eventually came to Ballarat. After the rebellion, he entered parliament and became a prominent politician.

NEW ZEALAND

It was British explorer Captain James Cook who called this part of the world 'The Great Britain of the South'. It consists of three islands, which were originally named after Irish provinces by a Waterford man who was the first governor of New Zealand, William Hobson. He called the Northern Island 'New Ulster', the Middle Island 'New Munster', and Stewart's Island 'New Leinster'.

Although the Irish were not the biggest immigrant group here, during the peak period of Irish immigration in the 1860s one-fifth of New Zealand's foreign population was Irish. There were two distinct streams of Irish migration: Protestant people came from Ulster as the British Government vigorously recruited future settlers from the north of Ireland by placing advertisements in Belfast and Londonderry, and Catholics came from Munster. Although in general they were Catholic, there were some periods during which more Protestant and elite Anglo-Irish people from Ulster looked for a fresh start there, for example during the time of Catholic emancipation and the rise of Irish nationalism, both of which made their situations in Ireland vulnerable. Throughout the nineteenth and twentieth centuries, Protestant immigrants were constantly arriving in New Zealand up until the 'Troubles' of the 1970s. It is estimated that about 15 per cent of the current population is of Irish descent.

In general Irish immigrants in New Zealand were slightly older, more financially secure and had a more mature outlook on life compared to those who settled in Australia. They generally came to New Zealand via Australia, which was a more populated and developed country at the time. Although New Zealand had never been a penal colony, some of the earliest immigrants included escaped prisoners or freed former convicts from Australia, sailors who had deserted and other fugitives.

When gold was discovered in New Zealand, hundreds of thousands of Irish gold miners in Australia made the move. During the Otago Gold Rush, which started in 1861, more than 50,000 gold seekers arrived from Australia or elsewhere. The discovery of gold in Hokitika on the West Coast also attracted a huge crowd. Many people left when the rushes subsided but some stayed and created vibrant new communities in New Zealand. Waves of Irish people who had once emigrated to South Africa also re-settled here.

The Kitikati settlement was established by an Irish farmer, coloniser and politician, George Vesey Stewart (1832-1920), a Trinity College graduate from Martray, County Tyrone. The settlement was on land that had been confiscated from the Māori after the Land Wars. As a result of his efforts, approximately 4,000 tenant farmers moved to New Zealand from County Tyrone. As its population grew, the region eventually developed into a thriving farming region.

As they had done elsewhere, Irish women worked as domestic servants and men worked as gold miners and navvies. Once they settled, they took up more permanent, secure jobs in the public sector such as the police force. Around the turn of the twentieth century, nearly half of the people in the police force were Irish Catholics. High-profile police commissioners include John Branigan, John Cullen and John O'Donovan.

Mayo man Sir Charles Christopher Bowen (1830-1917) was educated at Cambridge University. He emigrated with his family to the Canterbury settlement. With his legal training, he eventually became secretary to John Robert Godley, founder of the Canterbury colony, who was from Dublin. Bowen was in charge of the police force and was later involved in the first Canterbury Provincial Council before becoming Minister of Justice. He was responsible for creating compulsory, free, secular primary education for all.

Although discrimination against Catholics was not extremely vicious in New Zealand, they were somewhat underprivileged and were only allowed political representation in 1829. On a small scale, 'No Catholics Need Apply' or 'No Irish Need Apply' signs existed in newly established Protestant-dominated towns. Under the British system, as was the case elsewhere in the world, there were always reasons for the development of Irish nationalism. The Fenians and other independent groups that sought land reform were active during the mid-nineteenth century. High-profile Irish nationalist politicians traditionally visited their foreign counterparts for political, moral and financial support. John and William Redmond, John Dillon and Michael Davitt all visited New Zealand after Irish immigrants formed the Land League, the forerunner to the Irish National Leagues.

Since the 1860s, the Irish in New Zealand have been celebrating St Patrick's Day. Many Irish groups and associations also started mushrooming around the same time. Hibernian societies were established in Greymouth in 1869. Although at one point eighty-four branches all across New Zealand existed, they didn't merge to become a powerful mainstream institution.

Assisted immigration

Initially, New Zealand attracted very few people and almost none came from Ireland during the Great Famine. One reason for this was that the journey was long and expensive – in the mid-nineteenth century passage fees were four times higher to reach New Zealand than North America. Also, people wanted to emigrate to more attractive and familiar countries such as the US and Canada. Located in a remote region, New Zealand didn't have a good reputation either. It was known as a home of bloodthirsty cannibals and it was associated with the convict settlements of Australia. In order to populate the country, some incentives were needed.

Nobody went to New Zealand directly; usually they had to travel via the UK, Australia, South Africa or even the US. Often male children in a family moved there first and other family members followed them later in a chain migration. Dozens of assistance schemes by the government and from the private sector existed to attract immigrants and populate the country, but they were rather choosy – illiterate Irish peasants were not considered to be 'desirable immigrants'.

By 1851 Auckland had the biggest Irish population – around a third of the population were Irish immigrants. Three-quarters of these people had sailed from English ports or elsewhere, but the passenger lists contain a significant number of people whose country of origin is listed as Ireland.

In the mid-nineteenth century, with the help of the government of Canterbury, Irish people emigrated in droves to the province of Canterbury, which is located in the most central part of the Middle Island. The local authority wanted to develop a new settlement and build a railway and other infrastructure. The good pastures there meant some of the first settlers were sheep farmers from Australia who boarded the ships with their supply of livestock. A subsequent drought in Australia, which increased wool prices there, meant New Zealand's nascent wool industry became ever more attractive.

Catholic immigrants in the 1860s used the system of nomination to bring other family members. Many of those who used this scheme were from counties Kerry and Cork. Recruitment drives for potential settlers from Northern Ireland were also carried out systematically. As there was a need for domestic servants, single women were encouraged to emigrate. More Irish women than men came to New Zealand during the 1870s. The assisted emigrant scheme eventually died down due to the economic slump but was restored once again in 1904. Roughly a third of the Irish came from Australia and two-thirds from the UK during the early twentieth century.

At the beginning of 1871, the New Zealand Government started offering assisted passage to selected people through programmes such as the Waikato Immigration Scheme and the Vogel Immigration Scheme and there was a surge in the immigrant population during the decade, with many of the migrants coming from Ulster and settling in Pukekohe and Kawakawa.

Soldiers

Traditionally, there were more Irish than English soldiers in the British Armed Forces and early settlers in New Zealand included a substantial number of Irishmen who had once been soldiers. Some of them were discharged from British regiments and came to New Zealand while others came with the Royal New Zealand fencibles. The majority of the fencibles arrived between 1847 and 1852, accompanied by their wives and children. It is estimated that approximately 250,000 New Zealanders are descended from fencible families. The fencibles were basically soldiers who were recruited in Britain with attractive remuneration packages whose job it was to deal with the Māori and local settlers. The New Zealand Land Wars were a series of bloody battles that involved nearly 20,000 British troops, 2,500 Australian troops and 4,000 local Māori warriors. They spanned a couple of decades but the heaviest battles took place in the 1860s. After fighting against the Māori, many soldiers were discharged and settled in Auckland as they were given free land at the end of their service.

There were various Irish regiments, the first of which was the Christchurch Royal Irish Rifle Volunteers, which was established in 1868. A couple of regiments followed, such as the Canterbury Irish Rifle Volunteers, the Dunedin Irish Rifle Volunteers, the Southland Irish Rifle Volunteers, the Auckland Royal Irish Volunteers and the Irish Rifle Volunteers.

Catholicism

Patrick Moran was appointed the first bishop in Dunedin in 1869 and Thomas Croke became a bishop of Auckland in 1870. Since then, quite a few Irish bishops and archbishops followed in their footsteps. Although Irish associations and Gaelic cultural groups such as the GAA existed, they didn't take root in the most obvious way in New Zealand. This is because Irish immigrants identified more strongly with Catholic institutions rather than Irish institutions. Catholic schools, hospitals, orphanages and charities thrived in Irish communities.

The person who helped promote the astonishing growth of the Catholic Church in the region was the eminent bishop James Whyte (1868-1957). Born in County Kilkenny, he first moved to Sydney as a professor at St Patrick's College in 1892. He was the third Roman Catholic bishop of Dunedin between 1920 and 1957. He was responsible for establishing many parishes and St Kevin's College in Oamaru. During his time as bishop, the number of children attending Catholic schools sharply increased, as did the number of priests in the diocese. As a result, he was awarded the King George V Silver Jubilee Medal for his services.

The Orange Lodges

The first meeting of an Orange Lodge in New Zealand was held in 1843 and the movement soon became widespread all across the country. During the New Zealand Land Wars in the 1860s, the British troops brought a large number of future Orangemen as well as Catholic Irish people. A North Island Grand Lodge was established in 1867 and a South Island Grand Lodge was formed later, then the two merged in 1908. By the 1880s, forty-seven lodges with a couple of thousand members existed under the North Island Grand Lodge. In the nineteenth century, two-fifths of the Irish in New Zealand were Protestant.

As often happened elsewhere, there were frequent confrontations between Irish Catholics and Orangemen from their inception. In Christchurch in 1876, for instance, Catholic Irishmen attacked an Orange procession with pick handles and fighting broke out. Under the auspices of the Loyal Orange Institution of New Zealand, Howard Leslie Elliott founded the Protestant Political Association of New Zealand (PPA) in 1917. The association soon became powerful in many ways, which put Irish Catholics under threat. After the First World War and the Easter Rising, Catholic Irish immigrants became less interested in Irish nationalism, loosing much of their Irish identity, and identified themselves more with New Zealanders. Coincidentally, around the same time, Orangeism also began to fade away from the mainstream scene.

Politicians

New Zealand produced many Irish political leaders. They were responsible for shaping the political foundations and the national identity of the country. The country has had more than thirty prime ministers who have been Irish or of Irish descent.

Waterford man Captain William Hobson (1792-1842) initially joined the Royal Navy. After spending some time in Australia, he was sent to New Zealand in 1837 in order to deal with the Māori. He became the first British governor of New Zealand in 1841 when New Zealand became a Crown colony separate from New South Wales. He drafted the Treaty of Waitangi, signed by the British Crown and more than 500 Māori chiefs, making New Zealand a colony of Britain and, consequently, the Māori British subjects. Hobson picked the Waitemata Harbour for his capital, Auckland, as it was located in the midst of the dense Māori populations of the North Island.

Sir George Grey (1812-1898) was twice governor of New Zealand and the eleventh prime minister of New Zealand. He was born in Lisbon, Portugal. His father was an Irish solider, Lieutenant-Colonel Grey of the 30th Cambridgeshire Regiment of Foot, and his mother was the daughter of an Irish soldier who later became a clergyman. Grey initially went to Australia and became the third governor of South Australia. It was a difficult time in the colony as the British settlers treated the Aborigines in a horrendous way and, like many Irish people, he was sympathetic to them. He then moved to New Zealand and became governor of New Zealand from 1845 to 1853 and from 1861 to 1868, which was the time when the country was struggling with the Māori over their land and other rights issues. With his first-hand experience in Australia, he handled the Māori affairs sensitively. He was respected by Māori chiefs as he tried to learn their language, traditions and customs. He was one of the most influential politicians during the early years of New Zealand's history.

Dubliner Daniel Pollen (1813-1896) came to New Zealand via Australia. He worked as Commissioner of Confiscated Lands, under the Native Land Act of 1870 and immigration officer before he became the ninth premier of New Zealand.

Although James Edward Fitzgerald (1818-1896) was born in Bath, England, his parents were both Irish immigrants and he identified himself as an Irishman. Before arriving in New Zealand in 1850, he served as secretary of the New Zealand Canterbury Association in England. Like Ballance, he was aware of the importance of owning land and of being considerate of the local people's rights. He considered the land confiscations an enormous crime and suggested that Māori chiefs run the colony. He helped establish the Canterbury settlement and Christchurch city, and started, as well as edited, the first newspaper in Canterbury, *The Press*. He was one of the most notable pioneers, statesmen and orators in New Zealand.

Sir George Maurice O'Rorke (1830-1916) was known as one of the most dedicated politicians in New Zealand. Born in Moylough,

County Galway, he travelled to Melbourne after studying at Trinity College. He eventually settled in Auckland and started farming. After entering politics, he became a representative of Onehunga in Auckland, the eighth superintendent of the Auckland Province, Minister of Immigration and Crown Lands and councillor for the Auckland Provincial Council. Among other contributions, he did a significant amount of work to improve local education. Knighted in 1880, he served on the Legislative Council until his death.

The fourteenth prime minister, John Balance (1839-1893), was from Glenavy, County Antrim. After migrating to New Zealand and working as a shopkeeper and editor of the *Wanganui Herald*, he entered politics. He was the founder of the Liberal Party and shortly became Minister of Lands, Defence and Native Affairs, working hard to preserve law and order among the Māoris. He created the system of state-aided village settlements while supporting the rights of the indigenous people to keep the land they owned. As an Irishman, he knew first-hand what their land meant to them as the Irish had similar experiences of having their land taken from them. He was also responsible for the reduced military presence in Māori areas. In order to build a trusting relationship, he learned their language, history and culture.

After spending some time in Australia, Robert Thompson (1840-1922) from Newtown Butler, County Fermanagh, emigrated to New Zealand in 1870. He was a member of parliament for Marsden in Northland, New Zealand, between 1887 and 1902. His contribution included regional development and infrastructure, which boosted the economic growth.

Cork man Sir Patrick Alphonsus Buckley (1841-1896) worked in various different professions – judge, statesman, lawyer, soldier – and travelled extensively. After emigrating to Australia and serving as Chief Justice of Queensland, he moved to New Zealand where he became a member of the Wellington Provincial Council. He then served as colonial secretary in the Stout-Vogel Government as well as the Balance Government and also became Attorney General.

The nineteenth prime minister, William Ferguson Massey (1856-1925), was born in Limavady, County Londonderry. After emigrating to New Zealand, he worked on a farm in Auckland. He eventually became the opponent of left-wing movements and led a coalition government with Irish Catholic Joseph Ward during the First World War. After becoming prime minister, one of the first things he did was to authorise Crown tenants to buy their own farmlands.

Literature

As for literary accomplishments, Thomas Bracken (1843-1898) was a renowned literary figure. Born in Clones, County Monaghan, he was sent to Australia to join his uncle after he lost his parents as a child. He eventually moved to Dunedin in New Zealand where he published his first poetry and wrote the national anthem of New Zealand. He was the first person to use the phrase 'God's Own Country' in reference to New Zealand. He also worked as editor and writer for various local newspapers such as the *Otago Guardian*, *New Zealand Tablet* and *Morning Herald*. Over the years, he published several books, including some about the Māori. As a supporter of Governor George Grey, he defended local people's sovereignty and condemned the government's breaches of the Treaty of Waitangi.

Another notable and prolific writer is David McKee Wright (1869-1928) who was born in Ballynaskeagh, County Down. He was a gifted writer and poet who became well known in New Zealand and Australia. After arriving in New Zealand in 1887, he published four volumes of ballads, *Aorangi and other Verses* (1896), *Station Ballads and other Verses* (1897), *Wisps of Tussock* (1900) and *New Zealand Chimes* (1900). He moved to Sydney and carried on working as a freelance writer for various newspapers. He famously used pen names such as Pat O'Maori and Mary McCommonwealth.

7

ASIA

JAPAN

The first recorded Irish visitor to Japan was a sailor from County Waterford, Robert Jansen, who arrived on the southern island of Japan in 1704. He had fled the Dutch East Indies, or modern-day Indonesia, with five other foreign nationals, but the suspicious foreigners were immediately put in jail by samurai and eventually deported back to the Dutch East Indies.

Japan had been a country with a relatively functional government and a hard-working population. Catholic missionaries, particularly from Portugal and Spain, visited the country with the intention of spreading Catholicism but their efforts were not successful. This, combined with the activities of foreign traders, annoyed the Japanese Government, prompting it to take extreme measures by imposing a closed-country policy to control foreign trade activities and overseas influence. Thanks to their isolated geographical location, the Japanese have always managed to maintain their independence.

After more than two centuries of self-imposed isolation, Matthew Perry, a commodore of the US Navy of Irish descent, successfully negotiated with the Japanese Government to open the country in 1853, despite the fact that dozens of foreign delegates before him had failed. Japan opened its doors to foreign trade and diplomatic relations and foreign citizens were able to visit and reside in Japan. The time between the later years of the Edo era (1603-1868) and the early Meiji era (1868-1912) was a period of vibrant transformation when the Japanese Government wanted to modernise the country, which had previously been an isolated feudal society. To catch up with the Western world, the local authorities made an effort to hire foreign advisors, quite often directly employed by the government to work in important industry roles and academic institutions. During this progressive period when rapid changes in Japanese society affected its foreign relations and people's mind-set, nearly 10,000 overseas experts, two-thirds of them from Britain, had arrived in Japan by 1900. They successfully aided the modernisation process and contributed to the technical and industrial development of the country.

Although the majority of the people who came were British, American, French or German, quite a few Irish people visited, worked and settled in Japan. The Irish who went to Japan during this period were mostly British subjects and were highly educated and well-trained professionals. Some of them had specialised knowledge and arrived in Japan independently while others came as members of the British Foreign Service.

The most famous historical Irish figure in Japan is no doubt Patrick Lafcadio Hearn (1850-1904), who is better known by his Japanese name Koizumi Yakumo. He is one of the most highly distinguished English-language writers of all time and is partly responsible for introducing Japan to the world. He was a great storyteller and interpreter of Japanese culture. His father, Charles Bush Hearn from County Offaly, was the surgeon major in the British Army, who was stationed in Lefkada, Greece, during the British occupation, where he met his Greek future wife. Patrick was born in Lefkada but when he was two years old, his parents separated and he was brought back to Rathmines, Dublin, to live with his aunt. Paddy, as he was called as a child, grew up listening to the Celtic legends and myths, enjoyed being surrounded by nature and looked forward to spending long summer holidays in Tramore, County Waterford, and Cong, County Mayo, every year. As his father went abroad to work and his mother moved back to Greece, he had a lonely childhood that profoundly affected the formation of his personality, particularly his childhood penchant for creating imaginary worlds.

After studying in England, he moved to the US where he worked as a journalist. He established his writing career in Cincinnati, New Orleans, and Martinique in the West Indies before coming to Japan on journalistic assignments. Before long, he married the daughter of a samurai, adopted Japanese citizenship and acquired a Japanese name. He also taught literature at the Imperial University of Tokyo and wrote a significant number of books on Japan. He observed all aspects of his adopted land in a detailed and meticulous manner – from the political transformation of Japan to ghosts, fairies, insects and plants. He was also good at drawing and his pictures often accompanied his writing.

During the same period, William George Aston (1841–1911) was vigorously involved in the study of Japanese history and language. Born in Londonderry, he studied at Queen's University Belfast and later went to Japan with the British Foreign Service to work as a Japanese interpreter. As well as publishing comprehensive grammar and language texts, Japanese history and Shinto books, this major Japanologist had a thorough understanding of Japanese literature as he was completely fluent in written Japanese. After his death, Cambridge University Library obtained his substantial collection of rare Japanese books.

The first bandmaster in Japan and the author of the Japanese national anthem, the *Kimigayo*, was John William Fenton (1828–1890). Born in Kinsale, County Cork, Fenton initially went to Japan with the British Army in 1868. He soon began training for the brass band for soldiers in Yokohama, which developed into the nation's first military band. When the Emperor Meiji paid a visit to inspect the troops, the military band played the ceremonial melody of the national anthem for the first time in public. It had been composed by Fenton in collaboration with a local artillery captain. Although Fenton's regiment left Japan in 1891, his expertise was so valuable and beneficial to the band that he was asked to stay for another couple of years as a bandmaster for the newly formed Japanese Navy and the imperial court. He made a substantial contribution to the development of the Imperial Palace Music Department and is affectionately called the father of band music in Japan.

Ginza is one of the most expensive districts in Tokyo and it has always been the bustling city centre of the capital. It was the Irishman who modernised the area by designing and westernising it. Civil engineer and architect, Thomas James Waters (1842-1898) from Birr, County Offaly, was working on the buildings for the Royal Mint in Hong Kong when a British merchant, Thomas Blake Glover, who resided in Nagasaki at the time asked Waters to design western-style buildings in Japan. Waters agreed and initially came to Kagoshima in the southern part of Japan. After being hired by the government, he built the new Imperial Japanese Mint in Osaka in 1868. Upon completion, he was invited to Tokyo to officially take up his position as a foreign advisor. He worked on a variety of projects such as the Takebashi Barracks, a branch of the Japanese Mint in Ginza and numerous bridges. Already an accomplished engineer and architect, he made a remarkable contribution after the Ginza district was destroyed by fire in 1872. He laid out and rebuilt the brand new Ginza- (Georgian) style brick buildings with roads separated into a vehicle zone and a pedestrian sidewalk, lined with gas lamps and trees. This was influenced by the architecture of Dublin and was considered a symbol of the modernity and enlightenment of the Meiji era.

Another outstanding engineer was Dubliner Charles Dickinson West (1847-1908). The father of mechanical engineering in Japan spent many years mentoring future engineers. A graduate of Trinity College, he worked in shipbuilding, steel and steam engineering firms in the UK before moving to Japan in 1882 to take up a position offered to him by the Japanese Government. He arrived in Japan to become professor of mechanical engineering and naval architecture at the prestigious Tokyo University. As a well-respected and popular professor, he genuinely loved teaching and Japan. As well as teaching, he was involved in countless engineering projects, such as the Naval Architectural Department of the Imperial Navy, the Mitsubishi Dockyard, the Kawasaki Dockyard and the Osaka Iron Works. Hundreds of foreign advisors were hired in those days and they typically left after three to five years when their contracts ended. But West settled in Japan for the rest of his life. He eventually caught pneumonia while staying at the Atami hot springs and died shortly thereafter. He was buried in Aoyama Cemetery, Tokyo, where many other former foreign advisors rest forever. To honour his contribution, a bronze monument was unveiled in 1910 on the Tokyo University campus.

Another distinguished expert on Japan was Francis Brinkley (1841-1912). He was a military advisor, scholar and journalist. Born in County Meath, he started a military career after studying at Trinity College and became an artillery officer at the Royal Military Academy. He first visited Nagasaki in 1866 on the way to Hong Kong. Brinkley was moved when he saw a duel between two samurai – when the victor had slain his opponent, he covered him and knelt down with his hands clasped in prayer. Brinkley saw great respect in the conduct of samurai and Japanese culture. He eventually moved to Japan as an officer in the Royal Artillery and was later hired as a foreign advisor. He taught artillery techniques to the Imperial Japanese Navy and also lectured in mathematics at the Imperial College of Engineering. After marrying the daughter of a samurai, he immersed himself further in Japanese culture and language. He became the owner and editor of the *Japan Mail* newspaper and was also the foreign correspondent for *The Times* of London. As he was passionate about Japanese culture, he was involved in a wide range of Japanese cultural activities, such as pottery, arts, gardening and hunting. He published a variety of books on Japanese history, art and the Japanese language, including an English-Japanese dictionary. Writing was his vocation. His last work was on a *hara-kiri*, which is a Japanese ritual suicide that involves stomach-cutting with a samurai sword.

Born in Northern Ireland, William Willis (1837-1894) studied medicine in Glasgow, Scotland. He came to Japan as a medical officer with the British delegation. After working as the head of military operations, he became a professor at the faculty of medicine at Tokyo Imperial University and Kagoshima University. He played a key role in the field of medicine and mentored future medical doctors for fifteen years.

When Revd William Thomas Grey (1875-1968) from Dublin came to Japan as a missionary and lecturer at Keio University, the former Trinity College hockey star didn't give up playing his favourite sport. The veteran hockey player started teaching it to his students so that he could play with them. As a result, he produced countless high-level hockey players, earning him the title of the father of hockey in Japan.

Along with those distinguished, high-profile people, hundreds of Irish nuns and priests lived and taught in Japan although they may not have been very visible in this non-Catholic country. They had been settling in Japanese cities and towns to run schools and other institutions without converting people to Catholicism since the late nineteenth century. The universities that Irish missionaries established or traditionally taught at include: Elisabeth University of Music, Nagasaki Junshin Catholic University, Notre Dame Seishin University, St Catherine University, St Marianna University School of Medicine, St Thomas University, Kyoto Notre Dame University, Nanzan University, Seisen University, Shirayuri Women's University, Sophia University and the University of the Sacred Heart. Established in Ireland in 1916, the Missionary Society of St Columban started sending missionaries to Japan after the Second World War and scores of Columbans were sent to run the parishes all across Japan.

When the US Army dropped an atomic bomb on Hiroshima on 6 August 1945 during the Second World War, Irish nun Julia Canny (1893-1987), known as Sister Isaac Jogues, from Upper Kilbeg, County Galway, was in the city. She had been sent to Japan by the Society of the Helpers of the Holy Souls in New York, a US organisation. When the war started, she was immediately put in jail by the local authority. It took seven months before she was freed as she had to prove that she was not an American but an Irish national – Ireland was neutral during the war. When the bomb was dropped near her convent, she was saying a morning prayer outside. Miraculously, she survived and spent the rest of her life serving her mission in Japan.

Three days later, the US dropped another atomic bomb. This time, it was an Irish-American Major General Charles Sweeney from Lowell, Massachusetts who was responsible for dropping it on Nagasaki. Aidan MacCarthy (1914-1995) from Castletownbere, in west County Cork, was a medical doctor with the Royal Air Force being held as a prisoner-of-war in Nagasaki when it was dropped and black rain started falling over him. He was one of thousands of Irish men who fought for the Allies during the Second World War. After surviving the ordeal and the war, MacCarthy went home to Ireland.

INDIA

As had happened in Ireland, India rebelled against British rule and fought for freedom. Irish nationalist leaders, including Éamon de Valera, were in close contact with their Indian counterparts in order to provide moral support. While a significant number of Irish people passing through this part of the British Empire fought gloriously, made fortunes, became famous and infamous for their actions, a substantial number of them succumbed to the heat and tropical diseases and died without achieving their dreams.

Early Irish visitors to India were either soldiers in the British Army or involved with the East India Company, which was established in 1600. It was a London-based English trading firm that dealt in silk, cotton, spices, salt, tea, opium and so on. It also had its own private armies in which a great number of Irish people served.

By the nineteenth century, waves of Irish visitors and settlers had arrived with the British as academics, missionaries, and medical, geological and engineering professionals to develop local communities and infrastructure. By 1860, approximately 30 per cent of the engineers with Trinity College degrees got a job in their field in India. They were indispensable in building water systems, railway lines and other engineering projects.

Through trade, quite a few Irish people made a considerable fortune. James Alexander (1730–1802) moved to Madras, where he worked as an accountant before eventually becoming one of the wealthiest merchants in India at that time. He was also involved with the East India Company's civil service in Bengal. With the large amount of money he made, he bought vast stretches of land and the estate of Caledon in County Tyrone, becoming the 1st Lord Caledon. He also sat in the Irish House of Commons.

While working as an East India merchant, Robert Gregory (1727-1810) from County Galway also became prosperous in India. On returning to London, he became a director of the East India Company. He invested in land in Essex and Cheshire, bought the Coole Park estate in County Galway and built a house. He became a member of parliament for Maidstone and Rochester, England. His grandson is William Henry Gregory (1817-1892) who married the well-known writer Isabella Augusta Persse, better known as Lady Gregory (1852-1932). She notably transformed her home into a focal point of the Irish literary revival movement.

In 1796 Arthur Wesley, or the Duke of Wellington (1769-1852), arrived in India where his brother Richard was governor. As colonel, he took part in the Mysore War against Tipu Sultan. He is also known for hunting down a Maratha warlord.

Another high-profile officer was Robert Rollo Gillespie (1766-1814) from County Down. He commanded a couple of Irish brigades, such as the 19th Light Dragoons.

Irishmen served extremely well in the British Army, fighting a wide range of battles, such as the Indian Mutiny (1857-1858). For their remarkable contributions, numerous Irish soldiers were recognised and received the Victoria Cross medal. Among them were James McGuire (1827-1862) from County Fermanagh, Thomas Duffy (1806-1868) from County Westmeath, Stephen Garvin (1826-1874) from County Tipperary, Richard Fitzgerald (1831-1884) from County Cork, John Ryan (1823-1858) from County Kilkenny, Edward Jennings (1820-1889) from County Mayo, Thomas Henry Kavanagh (1821-1882) from County Westmeath, John McGovern (1825-1888) from County Cavan, George Forrest (1800-1859) from Dublin, Peter Gill (1831-1868) from Dublin, to name a few.

One of the most outstanding combat leaders in history was Frederick Sleigh Roberts, 1st Earl Roberts (1832-1914). Born in Cawnpore, India, to parents from counties Waterford and Tipperary, he served in various wars and conflicts all across the world, but it was during the suppression of the Indian Mutiny that he distinguished himself and received the Victoria Cross.

London-born Sir Charles James Napier (1782-1853) came from a notable military family from County Meath. He conquered the Sind

Province, which is modern-day Pakistan, and served as its governor. He established a police force, water-supply facilities in Karachi and trade routes and he was the British Army's commander-in-chief in the Second Sikh War (1848-1849) in India.

Walter Richard Pollock Hamilton (1856-1879) was born in Inistioge, County Kilkenny. He became lieutenant in the Indian Army's Corps of Guides. He commanded two squadrons during the Second Anglo-Afghan War at Futtehabad in Afghanistan. After the victory of Britain, he received the Victoria Cross.

Tipperary man Sir Michael O'Dwyer (1864-1940) was the lieutenant governor of Punjab between 1913 and 1919. He is considered one of the most notorious colonial officers in the history of the British Raj (1858-1947). Not only did he impose martial law in 1919, he also endorsed Brigadier-General Reginald Dyer's Jallianwala Bagh massacre in Amritsar. Dyer's army fired on an unarmed crowd who were protesting the arrest of two leaders. It is estimated that up to 1,000 people were killed. Two decades later, O'Dwyer was shot dead in London by Udham Singh who had held a grudge against him for twenty-one years.

8

SOUTH AFRICA

Irish migrants gradually trickled into South African communities from the 1780s onwards. Even though levels of Irish emigration to South Africa were relatively low, there were up to 18,000 Irish immigrants in the country by the turn of the twentieth century. Many of them benefited from various assisted migration schemes. However, this country has never been the most popular destination for the Irish and quite a few who did go there eventually left for Australia, New Zealand, South America or elsewhere. The majority of Irish migrants who settled in South Africa were middle class, slightly older, skilled and relatively well off.

As in New Zealand, Irish settlers lost their Irish identity fairly quickly in South Africa. Being in a completely unfamiliar setting certainly blurred the ethnic and cultural distinctions and Irish immigrants forged a new sense of South African identity. This was helped by the fact that they tended to marry non-Irish people in South Africa. Irish organisations and associations, as well as family and cultural networks, did not take root the way they did in the US. While various catastrophic attempts were made to settle Irish immigrants in rural regions, in general the Irish population was scattered throughout the country, though Irish communities always existed. In most cases, the Irish in Ireland felt that South Africa was too foreign and they didn't know much about the country, so chain migration didn't become a defining feature of the Irish community in South Africa.

SOLDIERS

The British established the Cape colony in 1806 and Natal in 1842. In order to enforce security for their colonies, permanent British garrisons were installed in those regions.

Before the Second Boer War (1899-1902), there were six Irish regiments: the 6th Dragoons (Inniskilling); the 8th Lancers (King's Royal Irish); the 27th Regiment of Foot (Inniskilling), the 83rd Regiment of Foot (County Dublin); the 86th Regiment of Foot (Royal County Down); and the 88th Regiment of Foot (Connaught Rangers). The earliest was the 86th Regiment of Foot, which was originally established in 1795 and became the Royal Irish Rifles, then the Royal Ulster Rifles and eventually affiliated with the South African Irish Regiment officially founded in 1914 at the outbreak of the First World War.

BUSINESS PEOPLE

One of the main characteristics of South Africa is that a large number of people arrived there with the intention of being their own boss. From small to large business and shop owners, there was no shortage of prosperous Irish immigrants.

A ship owner and trader, Henry Nourse from London, England, and John Ingram from County Cork brought a group of Irish people to settle in South Africa in 1820. Most of the early Irish newcomers settled in Cape Town, Port Elizabeth, Kimberley and Johannesburg. The brothers John and Joseph Orr from Benburb, County Tyrone, were accomplished businessmen. After arriving in South Africa in 1883, the two brothers established a chain of retail stores. Their first shop was opened in Cape Town, after which a John Orr & Co. shop was opened in Kimberley. John's contribution to society was well acknowledged and he eventually became mayor of Kimberley. After making substantial profits, he purchased the 1897 colonial mansion in Kimberley and called it Dunluce, which is the name of the famous castle in County Antrim.

William Cuthbert (1859-1916), a Protestant Irishman from Dungiven, County Londonderry, came to South Africa in 1881.

When the first shoe shop he opened was successful, he kept expanding and eventually owned seventy shops.

Another Ulster man, R.H. Henderson, who was from a Protestant family, was also an accomplished businessman in the retail industry. After arriving in 1884, he set up his first shop in Kimberley in 1887. As his business flourished, he opened branches all over the country. He was interested in politics and also served as mayor of Kimberley.

Other Irish immigrants, Mr McCullagh and Sam Bothwell, started a business selling men's clothing, shoes and school uniforms. Their first shop, McCullagh & Bothwell, was opened in Kimberley in 1896. A Limerick man, Frederick York St Leger (1833-1901), was the founder and editor of the first daily newspaper in South Africa, the *Cape Times*. The Dubliner Philip Maurice Dudgeon (1852-1891) was a prolific architect and after arriving in Natal, he quickly earned a reputation for being the best architect there. He did work for the Natal Government, as well as numerous other clients. Most famously, he designed the Standard Bank in Pietermaritzburg, which was based on the Bank of Ireland in Belfast. He also designed the town hall in Durban and Maritzburg College.

Another motive for people to migrate to South Africa was the mines. When diamonds were discovered in 1867 and gold in 1886, waves of Irishmen swarmed to the country to work in the mines. There were some Irish mining communities in Kimberley, Witwatersrand and Pilgrim's Rest, and dozens of Irish immigrants struck it rich in the mines.

Working for the police was also a popular choice for Irish settlers. They had a strong presence in some early police units called the Frontier Armed and the Mounted Police Force. The Natal Police was established in 1874 and later changed its name to the Natal Mounted Police. Established in 1882, the Cape Police, which later became the Cape Mounted Police (CMP), also had a workforce dominated by Irishmen. The first commandant was Major John Dartnell of the 27th Inniskilling and the first trooper was Edward Babington from Londonderry. Nearly 30 per cent of Irish immigrants were recruited in Ireland and the police paid for their third-class fare on a Union Castle liner. They were also notably in the Water Police in Durban and the Natal Government Railways' police force. Andrew Trimble from Fermanagh helped establish the Transvaal detective force in 1894.

POLITICIANS

Despite the fact that Irish people only represented a small proportion of the population, their presence in politics was overwhelming. A third of the Cape's governors were Irish and both the Cape and Natal colonies had scores of Irish politicians and colonial administrators, including some prime ministers. Being able to speak English and their understanding of the British system were certainly major advantages.

Known as the father of the Cape's constitution, William Porter (1805-1880) was attorney general of the Cape colony. Upon arriving in South Africa, the liberal Derry man was shocked at the racial sentiments of British settlers. He opposed land grabbing and adamantly believed that coloured people with appropriate qualifications should be eligible for jury duty. He pledged to promote equal rights for all and supported the idea of non-racialism in constitution-making. He was one of the primary drafters of the Cape constitution when the region was granted its first parliament in 1854. He had firmly believed that more Irish people should emigrate to populate South Africa and suggested it in the Cape's parliament. Later in life, he entered politics and promoted religious freedom, women's rights and the abolition of capital punishment. He was offered various honours and a knighthood in recognition of his contribution but he declined all of them. The town of Porterville in Western Cape was named in his honour.

The governor of Cape Colony between 1854 and 1861 was Sir George Grey (1812-1898). He founded Grey College in Bloemfontein and Grey High School in Port Elizabeth, and he also laid the foundation stone of the New Somerset Hospital in Cape Town. He donated a substantial personal collection of books and medieval and Renaissance manuscripts to the National Library of South Africa. His experience as governor of New Zealand, prime minister of New Zealand and governor of South Australia stood him in good stead in South Africa. In the same way he had handled the Māoris and Aborigines, he dealt with local affairs in South Africa with sensitivity and understanding.

After studying at Trinity College, and being called to the Irish Bar, Sir Thomas Upington (1844-1898) emigrated to the Cape Colony. The young Irish immigrant from Rathnee, County Cork, worked as Attorney General in the Gordon Sprigg administration. In 1884, he became prime minister of the Cape Colony and dealt with the conflict over two Boer mercenary states, Stellaland and Goshen in the British Bechuanaland, current Botswana. He was called the 'Afrikaner from Cork' as he was sympathetic towards the Boer states rather than taking strong action for the British. The town of Upington in the Northern Cape is named after him.

Sir Albert Henry Hime (1842-1919) from Kilcoole, County Wicklow, was a Royal Engineers officer in the British Army. He initially went to Bermuda to work on a causeway. As his work was greatly appreciated there, the well-respected Hime was sent to South Africa as a captain to be responsible for infrastructure such as roads, bridges, military outposts, piers, railways and the harbour. The capable engineer also built the Natal Mounted Police Headquarters. After serving as Minister of Lands, Works and Defence, he became the prime minister of Natal in 1899. As was the case with Upington, it was a difficult time to be in charge as he had to handle all kinds of indigenous troubles and conflicts, including Anglo-Boer war. With his engineering skills, he made himself extremely useful during the formation of the country. As a result of his enormous contribution, he was knighted and received awards. Himeville in KwaZulu-Natal is named in his honour.

The Irish nationalist and founder of Sinn Féin, Arthur Griffith (1871-1922), went to South Africa to join the Transvaal gold rush in 1897 and saw the plight of black people first-hand. He supported the cause of the Boers who fought against the British and admired Paul Kruger, the great figure of the Boer resistance. Using his experience as a printer and journalist, Griffith founded the weekly radical paper, *The United Irishman* in South Africa, which was first published in Dublin. *The Republic* was also established as the newspaper of the Irish

Republican Association of South Africa. During this period, all Irish nationalists were pro-Afrikaner. Former president of South Africa, Nelson Mandela (1918 -2013), who fought against apartheid, was an avid supporter of Sinn Féin and against IRA decommissioning.

MISSIONARIES

By 1860, quite a few Irish Catholic missionaries had been strenuously dealing with Irish settlers in South Africa, in particular in the Cape region. They were also involved in education, health and general pastoral work in remote areas where ordinary white people never set foot. Irish missionaries were especially active in the Eastern Cape, where all bishops who served in the nineteenth century were Irish. One of the earliest priests was Patrick Raymond Griffith (1798-1862), an Irish Dominican from County Wexford. After being made bishop, he came to the Cape of Good Hope in 1838 and served there until his death. His presence encouraged a few Irish communities that built up in his area.

As part of an effort to recruit English-speaking priests from Ireland to join the Society of African Missions, Father James O'Haire from Dublin was sent to South Africa in 1868. Another Dubliner priest, John Leonard (1829-1908), came to the Cape in 1872 and served as bishop until he died. Father O'Haire acted on behalf of Bishop Leonard. O'Haire came back to Ireland and recruited more missionaries to go to South Africa. In 1897, five sisters and four postulants from Our Lady of Mercy arrived in Cape Town. Sisters Mary Teresa Cowley, Magdalen Dunne, Evangelist McGlynn, Stanislaus Gallagher and Gonzaga McDonagh founded and opened the first Convent of Mercy in the diocese of Kimberley and later several convents were established in Johannesburg.

Although, there were more Protestant Irish than Catholic immigrants in South Africa, Orangeism didn't become hugely significant. The first lodge appeared in Cape Town in 1852, and there were twenty-six lodges during the peak period but they had all died out by the 1960s.

THE BOER WARS

The British Empire fought against the Dutch settlers, the Boers, over two Boer republics: the Orange Free State and the Transvaal Republic. The First Boer War (1880-1881) was a relatively small conflict and lasted for three months, resulting in a Boer victory. Irish soldiers were involved on both sides, fighting both for and against the British Empire, typically facing each other on the battlefield. One of the key commanders in the conflict was Major-General George Pomeroy Colley (1835-1881), from Dublin, who had been appointed to the Natal command in 1880.

The Second Boer War was a much larger and costlier one. Approximately 5,000 Irish soldiers, including the 500 Irishmen of the Driscoll Scouts, were involved on the British side along with a number of Irish nurses. Frederick Sleigh Roberts (1832-1814), whose father came from County Wexford, was in overall command of the British forces. One of the founders of the Imperial Light Horse Regiment was Irish South African, Sir James Percy FitzPatrick (1862-1931). He also served as official advisor on South African Affairs to the British Government.

Arthur Conan Doyle (1859-1930) also joined the Boer War, working as a volunteer doctor in Bloemfontein in 1900. He subsequently wrote a number of books on the Boer War such as *The War in South Africa: Its Cause and Conduct* and *The Great Boer War*. As they were positively received by the British Government, he earned the title 'Sir' after being knighted by King Edward VII.

About 500 Irish people and those of Irish descent from all across the world joined the battle against occupying British forces. Many Irish settlers in South Africa supported the leader of the Boers, Paul Kruger. There were two units of Irish commandos, the Irish Transvaal Brigade and the 2nd Irish Brigade. An Irish republican, John MacBride, organised the Irish Transvaal Brigade, which is also known as McBride's brigade. Its commander was Colonel John Blake, an Irish American. Irish Australian Arthur Alfred Lynch initially came to South Africa as a correspondent but ended up raising the Second Irish Brigade and became its colonel. Many Irish soldiers were experienced miners which meant they were good at handling dynamite, a skill they used to blow up railway bridges and facilities belonging to the British Army. As many Irish nationalists who had been fighting against the British in Ireland joined, the Boers called them *Het Wrekers Korps*, or The Avenging Corps.

The pro-Boer movement garnered support among Irish nationalists in Ireland. English-born Irish patriot Maud Gonne, in particular, organised all kinds of pro-Boer activities and went on to marry MacBride under the brigade's flag by the brigade's chaplain in Paris in 1903. The Irish nationalist and pro-Boer campaigner Michael Davitt came to South Africa on a journalistic assignment and wrote the publication *The Boer Fight for Freedom*, an analysis of the military campaigns and John Blake from his pro-Boer point of view. But the war ended with a British victory. Quite a few Irish soldiers remained in South Africa after the end of the war, although none of them received free land or any compensation after the service.

OTHER IMMIGRANTS

Although on a smaller scale than elsewhere, the British Government shipped some Irish convicts to South Africa during the Young Irelander Rebellion in 1848. However, the majority of Irish people in South Africa were voluntary immigrants. While typical Irish ghettos didn't exist in South Africa, some Irish towns and districts were formed, typically inhabited by working-class Irish people. For instance, railway construction workers built their own settlements along the railroad lines. In Newlands, Cape Town, a large number of Irish labourers who worked in Olhsson's Brewery formed their own settlement. So did constables and horse-drawn omnibus drivers in Woodstock, Cape Town. Countless dock workers created their own communities in various parts of Port Elizabeth and Durban. Throngs of Irish immigrants from Arklow, County Wicklow, were recruited to work and live at the Kynoch explosives factory in Umbogintwini, Durban.

Because of the distance, various emigration schemes existed throughout the nineteenth century. Quite a few Irish women were sent to marry former mercenaries; however, this plan didn't go smoothly and those girls and women ended up working as domestic servants. The first Irish brothel in town was formed after a group of single women were shipped to Cape Town.

9

EUROPE

FRANCE

Since the Middle Ages, Ireland has maintained a good relationship with Catholic Europe, especially France and Spain. As a result of the continuous movement of people in the region, France and Spain have attracted dozens of elite Irish immigrants. There were three immigrant groups that went on to occupy influential positions – in the fields of trade, the armed forces and the Church.

St Patrick's influence on Ireland was enormous. He didn't just bring Christianity to the country; he was also responsible for making it the isle of saints and scholars. Many monasteries were set up all across Ireland and these became places of study. During medieval times, Ireland was one of the most stimulating countries to be in for intellectually ambitious people. Irish scholars travelled to preach and helped establish institutions all across Europe. Early Irish Christian monks did much more than simply spreading Christianity; they played an essential role in the development of Western civilization during a time of turmoil and despair. Apart from preserving the Bible, they introduced the cultivation of crops, the brewing of beer, irrigation and other industries, as well as improving cattle breeds. They were pioneering wine producers, using the wine for both the Holy Mass celebration and daily consumption. They were also famous for being competent seafarers. As a result of the constant movement of people, Irish ports became more developed and Irish merchants and seafarers were seen in French, Spanish and other European ports.

Missionaries

French links with Ireland were established when Irish religious people moved to France during the early Middle Ages. Irish priests and nuns have been studying and helping to build the monasteries in France for centuries. The first Irish College was actually established in Spain and before long more than forty of them sprang up all across Europe, but the Irish College in Paris, which was established for Irish students in 1578 by Revd John Lee from County Waterford, became the most important of all of them. Students were able to take various courses, including theology, philosophy, medicine and law.

By 1700, various institutions were built for educating both the laity and clerical people in Paris, Nantes, Poitiers, Bordeaux, Toulouse, Bar-Sur-Aube, Wassy, Boulay, Douai and Lille. Thomas Gould (1657-1734) from County Cork had a great influence on the early Irish missionaries. After coming to France in 1678, he established himself at the Irish Jesuit College in Poitiers. He soon became an agent of the Catholic Bourbon monarchy, gaining the title *missionnaire du roi*, or king's missionary. He played a significant role in the Catholic Church in France and attempted to convert the Protestant Huguenot population to Catholicism.

Wild Geese

The term 'Wild Geese' refers to Irish mercenaries who fought in foreign armies, particularly on the continent. The last decades of the seventeenth century and the early eighteenth century were the peak periods of Irish military migration with many Catholic mercenaries joining Irish regiments or regiments that traditionally contained a high proportion of Irish men. The practice was so prevalent that Britain officially banned recruitment by foreign armies in Ireland in 1745.

The Irish regiments in the Spanish Army were well established and prevalent until around the mid-seventeenth century, but their numbers dwindled after this as joining the French Army became a more popular choice because France was spending more money on the recruitment of foreign soldiers to the military. The earliest systematic recruitment activity by the French Army started in 1635 when seven Irish regiments were formed in Ireland. The Wall family of Coolnamuck in County Waterford was hired to recruit local men and they successfully secured a large group of Irish soldiers who were promised they would be paid more than they would get in the Spanish Army. The wages of ordinary soldiers at that time were about the same as those of a peasant. Approximately 20 per cent of French troops were mercenaries during the eighteenth and nineteenth centuries.

The term Wild Geese actually dates from the Williamite Wars (1689-1691) which were fought between Jacobites, who were supporters of Catholic King James II, and Williamites, who were on the side of Protestant Prince William III of Orange. At stake was the throne of England, Scotland and Ireland. The Jacobites were defeated during the extremely bloody conflict. Under the Treaty of Limerick, if Jacobite soldiers wished to remain in Ireland, they needed to give an oath of loyalty to William and join the Williamite army. Approximately 1,000 joined the army in order to stay in the country.

When James II fled to France, up to 24,000 Jacobite soldiers left with him, taking their wives and children. This is called the 'Flight of the Wild Geese', which was the biggest Irish military migration.

As France's Louis XIV helped James II and the Irish Jacobites, a plethora of Irish soldiers fought for France during the Nine Years' War (1688-1697), between King Louis XIV of France and the Anglo-Dutch William III of Orange. At least 5,000 Irish soldiers sailed from Kinsale to Brest and enlisted for a minimum of six years. Justin McCarthy and Viscount Mountcashel both established Irish regiments in the French Army. There were three Mountcashel brigades – Clare, Dillon and Lee – under direct French control and ten regiments of foot, two regiments of horse and two horse troops of James II's Army.

Following the Treaty of Ryswick, which ended the Nine Years' War, Louis XIV agreed to recognise William of Orange as sovereign of Britain, and the French Army was reorganised to serve the French King. The infantry regiments comprised nearly 6,000 men and they were named after the colonel proprietors: Albermarle, Berwick, Burke, Clare, Dillon, Dorrington, Galmoy, Lee and so on. Commanded by Dominic Sheldon, the cavalry consisted of one regiment of two squadrons.

The Battle of Fontenoy, on 11 May 1745, was a large-scale battle in the War of the Austrian Succession which took place in southwest Belgium. France beat Britain, Austria and Holland. Tens of thousands of soldiers from the Irish regiments were involved. In this bloody battle, the soldiers were ordered to fight with fixed bayonets without firing. There were devastating mass casualties of Irish men. It is estimated that a quarter of the officers, including Colonel Dillon, and a third of the soldiers were killed.

The almost endless stream of Irish prisoners of war and British Army deserters joined to fight in the Seven Years' War (1756-1763), between Britain and the Bourbon Dynasty. The main Irish regiments during this war were Clare, Dillon, Rooth, Berwick, Bulkeley and Lally. Joining the French Army became a tradition for certain Irish families that settled in France.

During the French Revolution (1789-1799), Napoleon Bonaparte raised cavalry units called the Irish Legion, comprising the veterans of the Irish Rebellion of 1798. Count Paul Francois O'Neill, the French 5th Comte de Tyrone, was one of the notable soldiers who fought in the battle. There was a huge presence of Irish soldiers in Napoleon's Irish Legion during the Napoleonic Wars (1803-1815). Opposing military groups, as always, also contained a substantial number of Irish soldiers.

One of the most significant British Army officers was Arthur Wellesley, the 1st Duke of Wellington (1769-1852). Born into a well-to-do Anglo-Irish aristocratic family in Dublin, he was one of those people born in Ireland who wanted to be referred to as English rather than Irish. After serving for the British Army in Ireland, he climbed up the ranks to became a general in the Napoleonic Wars. As he once declared: 'Ireland was an inexhaustible nursery for the finest soldiers'. It will not come as a surprise then that his army always relied heavily on Irish military personnel. For instance, a third of his soldiers at the Battle of Waterloo in 1815 were Irish. As a proficient commander, he participated in sixty battles across the world, leading his army to many victories. He is considered one of the best defensive commanders in military history. Following his accomplished military career, he became a important member of the Tory party and prime minister of the UK from 1828 to 1830 and again briefly in 1834. As a former commanding officer, he treated everyone fairly. He played a leading part in the process of Catholic Emancipation in the UK, which sought to grant civil rights to Catholic people, as well as establishing King's College London. His brother Richard (1760-1842), the 2nd Earl of Mornington, was governor general of India.

Rollo Gillespie (1766-1814) was born in Comber, County Down. After studying at Cambridge, he joined the 3rd Irish Horse in the British Army, and commanded the 19th Light Dragoons. As an officer in the British Army, he experienced several arduous wars in various countries, including the French Revolutionary Wars.

The song 'It's a long, long way to Tipperary' was written by Jack Judge (1872-1938), whose grandparents were from County Tipperary and whose parents were from County Mayo. And it was John McCormack (1884-1945), an already internationally well-known Irish tenor from Athlone, County Westmeath, who first made it a popular military anthem during the First World War. This is definitely an immigrant's song or, to be more precise, an Irish mercenary's song. It was widely sung by Irish mercenaries. The Irish regiment, the Connaught Rangers', notably sang it as they marched along in France. The lyrics are as follows:

Up to mighty London came
An Irishman one day.
All the streets were paved with gold
So everyone was gay!
Singing songs of Piccadilly, Strand and Leicester Square
'Til Paddy got excited and
He shouted to them there:

It's a long way to Tipperary,
It's a long way to go,
It's a long way to Tipperary

to the sweetest girl I know!

Goodbye Piccadilly, farewell Leicester Square!

It's a long, long way to Tipperary

But my heart's right there.

Some other French connections include historically noteworthy official figures. A man of Irish descent, Patrice de MacMahon (1808-1893), became commander of the Foreign Legion and later president of France. Charles de Gaulle (1890-1970), the French general and statesman, had Irish ancestors on his mother's side: the MacCartans from County Down.

Statesman Seán MacBride (1904-1988) was born and grew up in Paris and never lost his thick French accent. His parents were Major John MacBride, who was executed in 1916 for his part in the Easter Rising against the British, and Maud Gonne, an English-born Irish revolutionary. As a former chief of staff of the IRA, he was imprisoned a couple of times for his IRA activities. After entering politics in 1946, he established various organisations, such as the political party Clann na Poblachta, or the Party of the Republic, and became Minister for External Affairs in the first interparty government. His international upbringing certainly helped make him more broadminded. He was also a founding member of Amnesty International. Through his humanitarian activities, he received the Nobel Peace Prize in 1974, the Lenin Peace Prize for 1975-1976, as well as the UNESCO Silver Medal for Service in 1980.

Slave traders

It is impossible to determine exactly what conditions were like for slaves but some historians claim that France was far more brutal than other countries and that far more slaves were shipped to the New World from France than from England and other slave-trading nations. France carried on the slave trade clandestinely even after it was made illegal.

Quite a few Irish people were actively involved in the slave trade. The French port of Nantes had become a large and established slaving port by the early 1700s. An Irish slave-trading community existed and half of the ships that sailed from Nantes during this period were owned by Irish people. Irish names such as Joyce, MacCarthy, Walsh, O'Sheil and Sarsfields were common in the lucrative slave trade, and slave ship captains and slave merchants in France made fortunes. The O'Riordan brothers, Etienne and Laurent, from Derryvoe, County Cork, sent out eleven expeditions between 1734 and 1749 and purchased more than 3,000 slaves. The Roches from County Limerick were another family involved in such activities.

France traded guns, textiles, liquor, knives and other manufactured products with the Slave Coast in West Africa and slaves were then shipped to the French colonies, such as Guadeloupe, Martinique and Saint Dominique, in exchange for sugar and tobacco.

With the profits of their business, the Irish slaver traders built many grand homes and other buildings in Nantes, especially on the Feydeau Island, and their hard work was recognised by French kings.

One of the most infamous Irish settlers in France was Philip Walsh. Born in Ballynacooley, County Kilkenny, he later settled in St Malo, Brittany. He was a captain in the French Navy. Philip and his French-born son Anthony Vincent Walsh (1703-1663), also known as Antoine, were in charge of the ship that carried the defeated King James II from Kinsale, County Cork, to France after the Battle of the Boyne. As a shipbuilder and merchant, he saw the profitable opportunity of taking part of the slave trade as irresistible. He was also a licensed pirate for the French Crown, which means he was able to legally attack and capture British ships on the English Channel.

Business people

France seems to have brought out considerable business acumen in Irish immigrants as they could be found in all fields. Two of the leading businessmen were Walter Rutledge, a merchant and ship owner in Dunkirk, and Richard Cantillon, who was a banker and economist in Paris. But the field that the Irish people most excelled in was the alcohol trade. The Irish invented some of the world's best wine and *eau de vie*, or brandy. As a matter of fact, pioneering Irish winemakers can be easily found not just in France but all around the world, including in the Napa/Sonoma valleys in California, US, the Clare Valley in Australia, and the Hemel En Aarde Valley in South Africa, to name but a few examples.

Thomas Barton (1694-1780) also made an outstanding contribution. After leaving Ireland for Bordeaux when he was 30 years old, this ambitious businessman first founded a wine-shipping company. The first barrels of wine were exported to his home country, Ireland. His wine was an instant hit and soon there were demands from all over the place. As the first Irish shipper to have his own wine estates, he acquired the nickname 'French Tom'. Later, his son William and grandson Hugh took over his wine business. In 1802, Hugh Barton teamed up with Daniel Guestier, a French trader, and established Barton & Guestier. It is one of the oldest wine merchants in Bordeaux. Other famous labels established by the Irish wine producers include: Château de Goulaine, Château Phélan-Ségur, Château MacCarthy, Château Lynch-Bages, Château Lynch-Moussas, Château Léoville-Barton, Château Clarke, Château Boyd-Cantenac and Château Dillon.

Hennessy is another Irish alcohol brand and the company is considered one of the world's finest cognac brandy makers. The Hennessy brandy label stems from Richard Hennessy (1724-1800), a former officer in the Dillon regiment of the Irish Brigade who fought for King Louis XV. After setting up his own brandy distillery in 1765 and building a great reputation in Paris and the royal court, he exported brandy to England and became world-renowned. The brand symbol is actually the Hennessy family coat of arms.

Writers

Paris is known as the city of enlightenment and has been home to some of the world's greatest intellectuals. In the nineteenth century, France offered an escape for Irish writers from the intellectually stifling political and social environment back home, where censorship and other restrictions applied. None of them returned to Ireland as their work would not have been sold there.

James Joyce (1882-1941) first moved to France as a young man to study medicine and later came back to Paris with his family to work on his novels. He also lived in other European cities. In total, he spent some twenty years in France. He wrote his masterpieces *Ulysses* and *Finnegan's Wake* in Paris. A life in exile as a struggling writer was rather gloomy. Fellow Irish immigrant Samuel Beckett, who was also trying to make ends meet, worked for him for a while. Too poor to pay for Beckett to continue doing his secretarial work, Joyce once gave him a pair of second-hand trousers in payment.

Joyce famously had a love-hate relationship with Dublin. He was outspoken about the Irish censorship and called Ireland morally and intellectually barren, although his books were never banned in Ireland. He said of his famous novel, *Ulysses*: 'I want to give a picture of Dublin so complete that if the city one day suddenly disappeared from the earth it could be reconstructed out of my book.' When he died in Zurich, his widow, Nora Barnacle, asked the Irish State to repatriate her husband's body to Ireland but her request was promptly denied.

Samuel Beckett (1906-1989) also left Ireland and never came back. The Dubliner spent most of his adult life in Paris, died there and was buried in the prestigious Montparnasse Cemetery in Paris. The recipient of the Nobel Prize in Literature in 1969, he wrote in both English and French. He learned from Joyce, his mentor, how to write and construct prose. Apart from being an outstanding playwright and novelist, he was also a courier for the French Resistance.

Although he didn't leave Ireland for France, Oscar Wilde (1854-1900) visited France on various occasions throughout his lifetime. He was fluent in French, having been taught it as a child in his Dublin home. The last part of his life – after he was imprisoned for the crime of sodomy and released from the jail in England in 1897 – was spent in exile, most of the time at Hôtel d'Alsace in Paris. Right after leaving England for France, he immediately wrote his magnum opus, 'The Ballad of Reading Gaol'. When he suffered from cerebral meningitis, a Dublin priest, Father Cuthbert Dunne, conditionally baptised him. He passed away soon afterwards and was buried in the Père Lachaise Cemetery in Paris.

Although he didn't stay long, Brendan Behan (1923-1964), the playwright and writer who wrote in both Irish and English, lived in Paris in the 1950s. In those days, he was a budding writer who embraced the artistic surroundings in France. One of his most-read books is *Borstal Boy*, an autobiographical account of his detention at Borstal, a young offenders' institution in England. Dublin-born Behan was sent there when he was just 16 after being arrested in Liverpool for bringing explosives into England for the IRA's bombing campaign.

SPAIN

The relationship between Spain and Ireland is not only diplomatically friendly but true and deep. In Irish mythology, the descendants of Milesians, or soldiers of Hispania, were actually the earliest settlers of Ireland. They were the Irish Gaels who spoke in a Celtic language. No one knows how true this is but the early settlers in Ireland are genetically related with the Spanish.

During the medieval period, Irish and Spanish ports were closely linked for commercial and fishing purposes. The ports of Waterford, Dublin, Limerick and Galway steadily traded with Bilbao, Cádiz, Lisbon and La Coruña. They exchanged fish, hides and timber for iron, salt, grain, wine, and so on. In particular, the trade in beef and leather between Galway and Spain flourished.

For centuries, the Irish have also been travelling to Spain as soldiers, diplomats, missionaries, merchants and students. With their shared religious beliefs the Irish naturally fitted in and Spain put their trust in Irish Catholics. Many Irish immigrants who became influential settlers in the Americas initially spent some time in Spain.

During plantations of Ireland in the sixteenth and seventeenth centuries when Catholic lands were confiscated, Spain welcomed hundreds of thousands of Irish settlers. Spain also financially helped establish Catholic colleges and institutions. The most notable institution in Spain was the University of Salamanca, where Irish archbishops, bishops, provincials of religious orders and other priests were traditionally educated. The Jesuit Thomas White of Clonmel established the Irish college, the Royal College of Saint Patrick for Irish Nobles, at Salamanca in 1592. Together with another Irish Jesuit, James Archer, he ran the institution and the Irish Jesuits were always in residence. Following the defeat by the British at Kinsale in 1602, parish priest of Fermoy, Eugene MacCarthy, moved to Santiago and set up the Irish College of Santiago de Compostela for Irish exiles in 1605. To train secular and diocesan clergy, a total of twenty-nine Irish colleges were built on the continent by 1689. The once vibrant Spanish church connections slowly disappeared at the end of the eighteenth century due to a series of external events, including the French Revolution, the politically motivated suppression of the Jesuits in Spain and the establishment of the National University of Ireland, Maynooth.

Ireland and Spain's military assistance was often reciprocal as they both sought to do the same thing – fight against England. After the failure of the Spanish Armada to overthrow Protestant England in 1588, Philip II of Spain (1527-1598) offered help to the Irish who were fighting against the English and welcomed a large number of Irish Catholic exiles to his kingdoms. Irish men serving in Catholic armies were not uncommon in those days. Spain traditionally hired a substantial number of Irish soldiers and most of the time they received good compensation and pensions for their service, including benefits for widows. The Irish soldiers gained a reputation for resilience and for fearlessly accomplishing their mission.

One of the earliest Irish regiments to serve for Spain was the Spanish Army of Flanders during the Eighty Years' War (1568-1648). An English Catholic, William Stanley, recruited this Irish regiment in Ireland. During the period of Irish self-government, which began after the Irish Rebellion of 1641, many of them returned to Ireland to fight for Confederate Ireland (1642-1649). When the Confederates lost the battle against Cromwell, tens of thousands of Irish Confederate soldiers fled to Spain. Some of them stayed in Spain, while others defected to join the French Army.

During the time when the old Gaelic order had almost ended, those chieftains who refused to obey the English rule sought refuge in the land of England's main enemy, hoping to fight back in the future. The most famous instance of this was the Flight of the Earls, which occurred on 4 September 1607, when Hugh O'Neill, the Earl of Tyrone, and Rory O'Donnell, the Earl of Tyrconnell, along with a close circle of family and supporters, got on a ship at Rathmullan on

Lough Swilly and set sail for La Coruña, Spain. On another occasion, more than 17,000 Irishmen went to Flanders, which was part of the Spanish Netherlands between 1623 and 1665. Eventually most of them were transferred to Spain.

Over the course of history, nearly 200 Irish generals served in the Irish regiments of the Spanish Army, such as the Regiment of Hibernia (or O'Neill's Regiment), the Irish Regiment, the Limerick Infantry Regiment, the Ulster Infantry Regiment, the Wauchop Infantry Regiment, the Waterford Infantry Regiment and the Dragoon Regiment of Dublin.

Born in County Armagh, Owen Roe O'Neill (1583-1649) had a significant military career in the Spanish Army. The son of Art MacBaron O'Neill and the nephew of Hugh O'Neill, Earl of Tyrone, he first joined during the Nine Years' War against the English in Ulster. After enlisting in an Irish regiment of the Spanish Army, he served with distinction and worked his way up the military ladder. He also distinguished himself by successfully leading a newly raised Irish regiment during the Franco-Spanish War (1635-1659).

A cousin of Juan MacKenna, who became a hero of the Chilean War of Independence, Field Marshall Alejandro O'Reilly (1722-1794) was born in Dublin. After joining the Spanish forces and fighting dozens of wars, he climbed up the top military rank and held various important and high-profile positions, such as Inspector General of Infantry for the Spanish Empire. He also served in Algeria, Cuba and Puerto Rico and became the first Spanish governor of colonial Louisiana in America. As his service for Spain was recognised and appreciated greatly, he earned the title of a *conde*, or count, and was granted a coat of arms.

The first Irishman to become Spanish prime minister was Richard Wall, or Ricardo Wall, (1694-1777). Born in Nantes, France, to Irish Jacobite parents from County Limerick, he led a distinguished military career in the Spanish Empire. He was eventually knighted with the Spanish military Order of Santiago and granted lordship of Peñausende (present-day Zamora and Salamanca provinces) in 1741. Another prime minister was Leopoldo O'Donnell (1809-1867). Born in the Canary Islands, he was a descendant of the O'Donnells who left Ireland after the Battle of the Boyne. After serving as an accomplished soldier and gaining fame, he served as prime minister of Spain three times. He became Duke of Tetuán, which is one of the most remarkable titles in Spain.

In more modern times, the Irish were heavily involved with the Spanish Civil War (1936-1939). It was a military revolt between the Republicans, who were conservative and loyal to the Spanish Republic, and the Nationalists, or the rebels led by General Francisco Franco. The Nationalists won and Franco ruled Spain for the next thirty-six years. It is estimated that approximately 7,000 Irish Catholic volunteers fought on the Spanish Nationalist side. Many of them were veterans of the Irish War of Independence. At the outbreak of the Spanish Civil War in 1936, the Irish brigade called the Connolly Column – named after the Irish republican James Connolly – was formed. It was the Limerick IRA man Frank Ryan (1902-1944) who led the Connolly Column.

Most of the Irish volunteers were somehow engaged in the Irish nationalist movement or the IRA. The brigade also included dozens of people from the Communist Party of Ireland. One of the high-profile volunteers was Robert Hilliard (1904-1937), a former clergyman turned Marxist and IRA member. He was shot dead in action.

Eoin O'Duffy (1892-1944) from County Monaghan also led the Irish brigade of 700 Irish soldiers to fight for Franco. Irish Socialist Volunteers were also formed to support Franco. The volunteers came from both Irish Republican and Unionist backgrounds but united with common socialist political ideology. In the mid-twentieth century, the IRA was linked with ETA (*Euskadi ta Askatasuna*, or Basque Homeland and Freedom), an armed Basque nationalist organisation, which has been fighting for freedom from the Spanish Government since 1959. Irish fighters found great similarity between the Irish and the Spanish struggle for independence and freedom.

Sherry makers

Sherry is a type of fortified wine that is produced in the Spanish town of Jerez, near the port of Cadiz. The Irish have proved to be some of the finest sherry producers in the world. One of the best-known sherry houses in Spain was established by Patrick Murphy, who started a sherry firm called the House of Domecq in 1730. An aristocratic farmer, William Garvey from County Waterford, created his own label, San Patricio Fino, in Jerez in 1798 and later the Esplendido brandy brand. He was the first person to systematically ship alcoholic drinks back to Ireland and his son developed his father's business into an internationally known enterprise. It was the Irish who were responsible for the growth of the export of sherry to all regions of Europe.

EPILOGUE

The title says it all: this book is an overview of the Irish diaspora in a nutshell. I've attempted to map out this expansive subject – on the where, when, why, who, what and how of Irish immigration. The book highlights the effect that the Irish had on culture, economy, politics, the military and so on in all countries where there was a significant Irish presence or high-profile Irish figures. I've tried to be objective and fair while researching the countries mentioned in the book, most of which I have travelled to.

When outside of Ireland, Northern Irish affairs still dominate news stories about Ireland. But the outlook of Northern Ireland together with the Republic has changed greatly over the last few decades. Above all, Ireland, both north and south, has become a migrant-receiving country. With a huge influx of immigrants from all parts of the world, it looks like Ireland has enough jobs to cater for all people. But the Irish themselves are scattering at an unprecedented speed. The Irish diaspora is not confined to the framework of history but in fact it is still as strong as ever. I've bumped into Irish priests and nuns, charity workers, journalists, business people, soldiers, nannies and builders in the remotest regions of the world, from Djibouti to Fiji.

Although it is well known that the Irish are all over the place, it was still quite staggering to experience the sheer scale of the Irish diaspora after researching it in detail. It is no exaggeration to say Irish immigrants and Irish descendants shaped the landscapes of many places, predominantly in English-speaking countries, as was the case in the US where they were a huge part of American Dream.

The Irish had to endure unimaginably atrocious experiences such as ethnic cleansing, the Great Famine and British control. As a consequence, millions of people left Ireland for a host of different reasons through the centuries. The difficulties experienced by the Irish had a transformative effect as it resulted in new identities based on democracy, equality and optimism. I was constantly reminded that the Irish people could be considered the ultimate survivors as they are the ones who seem to be 'most adaptable to change', to borrow Charles Darwin's words. They were not just capable politicians and business people but founding fathers, Hollywood icons, wine makers, Robin Hoods, architects, and their contribution is striking on all continents. We must also remember the countless Irish orphans, slaves, teenage soldiers and navvies who died before their time. In many cases, Irishness evaporates within an immigrant's lifetime as they integrate into their adopted lands. The Irish didn't have an official nationality of their own until the twentieth century anyway. The characteristics we associate with the Irish were no doubt formed during their long struggle for independence amid the sad and tragic cycle continued. The first thing you discover about the uniqueness of Irish people is their laid-back nature, sense of compassion towards the underprivileged, and their storytelling abilities.

Upon completion of this book, I took a long stroll along the River Thames. During this seemingly mundane late afternoon, I happened to notice, for the first time, a bust of Bernardo O'Higgins facing the water in Richmond. Of course he was here. He spent some of his formative years studying in this corner of the world, before becoming one of the founding fathers of Chile. I had stumbled into the past, serendipitously.

Miki Garcia
London, England, 2014

BIBLIOGRAPHY

Akenson, D.H., *The Irish Diaspora* (Toronto: P.D. Meany Publishers, 1996).

Asbury, H., *The Barbary Coast: An Informal History of the San Francisco Underworld* (New York: Thunder's Mouth Press, 1933).

Baines, D., 'The Economics of Migration: Nineteenth-Century Britain', *ReFresh*, 27, Autumn 1998.

Balarajan, R., 'Ethnicity and Variations in the Nation's Health', *Health Trends*, 27, 1995, pp. 114-9.

Barker, M., *More San Francisco Memoirs 1852-1899* (San Francisco: Londonborn Publications, 1996).

Barker, T., et al. (eds), *Population & Society in Britain 1850-1980* (London: Batsford Academic and Educational Ltd, 1982).

Barrett, A., 'Irish Migration: Characteristics, Causes and Consequences', *Institute for the Study of Labor (Germany) discussion paper series*, 97, 1999.

Bartlett, T. (ed.), *Irish Studies: A general introduction* (Dublin: Gill and Macmillan 1988).

Beckett, J., *The Anglo-Irish Tradition* (Belfast: Blackstaff Press, 1976).

Bedarida, F., *A Social History of England 1851-1975* (London: Methuen, 1976).

Belchem, J., *The Irish Diaspora: The Complexities of Mass Migration* (Liverpool: University of Liverpool Working Paper, 2005).

Black, J., et al., *Studying History* (Houndmills: Macmillan, 2000).

Boran, P., *A Short History of Dublin* (Cork: Mercier Press 2000).

Boyce, D.G., *The Irish Question and British Politics 1868-1996* (London: Macmillan, 1988).

Boyd, A., *The Rise of the Irish Trade Unions* (Dublin: Anvil Books, 1972).

Boylan, T., et al., 'Politics and Society in Post-Independence Ireland' in Bartlett, T. (ed.), *Irish Studies: A General Introduction* (Dublin: Gill and Macmillan, 1988).

Breen, R. (ed.), et al., *Understanding Contemporary Ireland: State, Class and Development in the Republic of Ireland* (London: Gill and Macmillan, 1990).

Brown, T., *Ireland: A Social and Cultural History 1922-79* (Glasgow: Fontana Paperbacks, 1981).

Brunt, B., *The Republic of Ireland* (London: Paul Chapman Publishing, 1988).

Bulmer, M., *Racism* (Oxford: Oxford Readers 1999).

Burca, M., *The GAA: A History* (Dublin: Gill and Macmillan, 1980).

Burchell, R.A., *The San Francisco Irish 1848-1880* (Los Angeles: University of California Press, 1980).

Cahill, Thomas, *How the Irish Saved Civilization* (New York: Random House, 1997).

Cairns, D., et al., *Writing Ireland: Colonialism, Nationalism and Culture* (Manchester: Manchester University Press, 1988).

Castles, S. (ed.) et al., *The Age of Migration: International Population Movements in the Modern World* (Houndmills: Macmillan, 1993).

Clout, H. *History of London* (London: Times Books, 2004).

Coakley, J. (ed.) et al., *Politics in the Republic of Ireland* (London: PSAI press, 1992).

'Commission on Emigration and Other Population Problems, 1948-54', *Reports* (Dublin: The Stationery Office, 1955).

Connor, T., *The London Irish* (London: London Strategic Policy Unit, 1987).

Coogan, T.P., *Ireland in the Twentieth Century* (London: Arrow Books, 2004).

Coogan, T.P., *Wherever Green is Worn: The Story of the Irish Diaspora* (London: Arrow Books, 2002).

Cowley, U., *The Men Who Built Britain* (London: Merlin Publishing, 2001).

Cronin, S., *Irish Nationalism: A History of its Roots and Ideology* (Dublin: Pluto Press, 1980).

Cross, I.B., *A History of the Labor Movement in California* (Berkeley: University of California Press, 1935).

Curran, M., *Across the Water: A Guide for Yound Irish People going to Britain* (London: Irish Chaplaincy in Britain, 1994).

Curtin, C. et al., 'Emigration and Exile' in Bartlett, T. (ed.), *Irish Studies* (Dublin: Gill and Macmillan, 1988).

Davis, G., *The Irish in Britain 1815-1914* (Dublin: Gill and Macmillan, 1991).

Deane, C., *The Guinness Book of Irish: Fact and Feats* (London: Guinness Publishing, 1994).

Delaney, E., *Demography, State and Society: Irish Migration to Britain, 1921-1971* (Kingston/Montreal and Liverpool: Liverpool University Press, 2000).

Delaney, E., *The Irish in Post-War Britain*, (Oxford: Oxford University Press, 2007).

Dolan, J.P., *The Irish Americans: A History* (New York: Bloomsbury Press, 2008).

Donoghue, F., *Defining the Nonprofit Sector: Ireland*, Working Papers of the Johns Hopkins Comparative Nonprofit Sector Project, Policy Research Centre at National College of Ireland, 1998.

Driscoll, C.B., *Kansas Irish* (London: Art and Educational Publishers, 1946).

Dowling, P.J., *Californians: The Irish Dream* (San Francisco: Golden Gate Publishers, 1988).

Dowling, P.J., *Irish Californians: Historic, Benevolent, Romantic* (San Francisco: Scottwall Associates, 1998).

Dunne, C., *An Unconsidered People: The Irish in London* (Dublin: New Island, 2003).

Dwyer, J.T., *Condemned to the Mines: The Life of Eugene O'Connell, 1815-1891: Pioneer Bishop of Northern California and Nevada* (New York: Vantage Press, 1976).

Dye, Alan et al., The Political Economy of Land Privatization in Argentina and Australia, 1810-1850 (Hawaii: Worknig Paper No. 12-7, University of Hawaii at Mānoa Department of Economics, 2012)

Eves, L., 'A History of California Labor Legislation with an Introductory Sketch of the San Francisco Labor Movement', *University of California Publications in Economics*, 1910, Vol. 2, pp. 338.

Ellis, P., *A History of the Irish Working Class* (London: Pluto, 1972).

Emmons, D.M., *Beyond the American Pale: The Irish in the West, 1845-1910* (Norman: University of Oklahoma Press, 2010).

Emmons, D.M., *The Butte Irish: Class and Ethnicity in an American Mining Town 1875-1925* (Urbana: University of Illinois Press, 1990).

Engstrom, D., *The Economic Determinants of Ethnic Segregation in Post-War Britain* (Yale University Working Papers, 1997).

Fahey, P., *The Irish in London* (London: A Centerprise Book, 1991).

Fallon, B., *An Age of Innocence: Irish Culture 1930-1960* (Dublin: Gill & Macmillan, 1999).

Ferriter, D., *The Transformation of Ireland 1900-2000* (London: Profile Books, 2004).

Fisk, R., *In Time of War: Ireland, Ulster and the Price of Neutrality 1939-1945* (Dublin: Gill & Macmillan, 1983).

Foster, R.F., *Modern Ireland 1600-1972* (London: Penguin Books, 1988).

Foster, R., *Paddy & Mr Punch* (London: Penguin Books, 1993).

Fraser, T.G., *Ireland in Conflict 1922-1998* (London: Routledge, 2000).

Friends of the Huntington Library, *Letter from a Gold Miner* (San Marino: Anderson & Ritchie, 1944).

Garcia, M., *The Irish in San Francisco after the Gold Rush* (New York: The Edwin Mellen Press, 2013).

Garrett, P.M., 'The Abnormal Flight: The Migration and Repatriation of Irish Unmarried Mothers', *Social History*, 25 (3), October 2000, pp. 330-343.

Garvey, J. et al., *Irish San Francisco* (Charleston: Arcadia Publishing, 2008).

Grant, C. (ed.), *Built to Last?: Reflections on British Housing Policy* (London: ROOF magazine, 1992).

Gray, B., *Breaking the Silence: Emigration, gender and the making of Irish cultural memory*, University of Limerick, Department of Sociology Working Paper Series, 2003.

Gregory, Adrian (ed.), *Ireland and the Great War: A War to Unite Us All?* (Manchester: Manchester University Press, 2002).

Handley, J.E. *The Irish in Scotland 1798-1845* (Cork: Cork University Press, 1943).

Harrison, G. *The Scattering: A History of the London Irish Centre 1954-2004* (London: The London Irish Centre, 2004).

Hickman, M.J., et al., *Discrimination and the Irish community in Britain* (London: Commission for Racial Equality, 1997).

Hickman, M.J., 'Reconstructing Deconstructing Race: British Political Discourses about the Irish in Britain', *Ethnic and Racial Studies*, 1 (2), 1998, pp. 288-307.

Holohan, A., et al., *Working Lives: The Irish in Britain* (Hayes: The Irish Post, 1995).

Hopkins, E., *The Rise and Decline of the English Working Classes 1918-1990: A Social History* (London: Weidenfeld & Nicolson, 1991).

Howarth, K., *Oral History* (Stroud: Sutton Publishing, 1998).

Howe, S., *Ireland and Empire: Colonial Legacies in Irish History and Culture* (Oxford: Oxford University Press, 2000).

Hughes, Robert, *The Fatal Shore: The Epic of Australia's Founding* (New York: Random House, 1988).

Hutton, S. (ed.), et al., *Ireland's Histories: Aspects of State, Society and Ideology* (London: Routledge, 1991).

Ignatiev, Noel, *How the Irish became White* (London: Routledge, 1995).

Ihde, W.T. (ed.), *The Irish Language in the United States: A Historical, Sociolinguistic, and Applied Linguistic Survey* (Westport, Connecticut: Bergin & Garvey, 1994).

Innes, C.L., *Woman and Nation in Irish Literature and Society, 1880-1935* (Hempstead: Harvester Wheatsheaf, 1993).

Jackson, J.A., *The Irish in Britain* (London: Routledge, 1963).

Jackson, J., *Migration* (Harlow: Longman Group, 1986).

Jessop, G., *Gerald Ffrench's Friends* (New York: Longmans, 1889).

Joppke, C., *Immigration and the Nation-State: The United States, Germany and Great Britain* (Oxford: Oxford University Press, 1999).

Jordan, D. (ed.), et al., *The Irish in the San Francisco Bay Area: Essays on Good Fortune* (San Francisco: Forbes Mill Press, 2005).

Jordan, D. (ed.), et al., *White Cargo: The Forgotten History of Britain's White Slaves in America* (New York: NYU Press, 2008).

Jordanova, L., *History in Practice* (London: Arnold, 2000).

Kazin, M., *Barons of Labor: The San Francisco Building Trades and Union Power in the Progressive Era* (Chicago: University of Illinois Press, 1987).

Kells, M., *Ethnic Identity Among Young Irish Middle Class Migrants in London* (London: University of North London, 1995).

Kelly, D., *I only came over for a couple of years…* (London: TG4, 2003).

Kenny, K., *The American Irish: A History* (New York: Longman, 2000).

Kenny, K., 'Diaspora and Comparison: The Global Irish as a Case Study', *The Journal of American History,* June 2003, pp. 134-62.

Kenny, K., *Making Sense of the Molly Maguires* (New York: Oxford University Press, 1998).

Keogh, D. *Twentieth-Century Ireland: Nation and State* (Dublin: Gill & Macmillan, 1994).

Langley, H.G., *Langley's San Francisco Directory 1858* (San Francisco: Francis, Valentine & Co., 1858).

Langley, H.G., *Langley's San Francisco Directory 1871* (San Francisco: Francis, Valentine & Co., 1871).

Langley, H.G., *Langley's San Francisco Directory 1880-1881* (San Francisco: Francis, Valentine & Co., 1881).

Langley, H.G., *Langley's San Francisco Directory 1895* (San Francisco: Francis, Valentine & Co., 1895).

Leavey, G., *et al.*, 'Older Irish Migrants Living in London: Identity, Loss and Return', *Journal of Ethnic and Migration Studies*, 30 (4), 2004, pp. 764-79.

Lee, J.J., *Ireland 1912-1985 Politics and Society (*Cambridge: Cambridge University Press, 1989).

Lees, L.H., *Exiles of Erin: Irish migrations in Victorian London* (Manchester: Manchester University Press, 1979).

Lennon, M., et al., *Across the Water: Irish Women's Lives in Britain* (London: Virago Press, 1988).

Lewis, P., *The Fifties* (London: Book Club Associates, 1978).

Lewis, W.A., 'Economic Development with Unlimited Supplies of Labour', *The Manchester School of Economic and Social Studies*, 22, 1954, pp. 139-91.

Lipsky, W., *Gay and Lesbian San Francisco* (San Francisco: Arcadia Publishing, 2006).

Lynch, A., *The Irish in Exile: Stories of Emigration* (London: Community History Press, n.d.).

Lynch-Brennan, M., *The Irish Bridget: Irish Immigrant Women in Domestic Service in America 1840-1930* (New York: Syracuse University Press, 2009).

Lynn, M. (ed.), *The British Empire in the 1950s: Retreat or Revival?* (Houndmills: Palgrave Macmillan, 2006).

Lyons, F. *Ireland Since the Famine* (London: Fontana Press, 1971).

MacAmhlaigh, D., *An Irish Navvy: The Diary of an Exile* (Cork: The Collins Press, 1964).

Mac an Ghaill, M., 'The Irish in Britain: The Invisibility of Ethnicity and Anti-Irish Racism', *Journal of Ethnic and Migration Studies*, 26 (1), 2000, pp. 137-47.

MacRaild, D., *Irish Migrants in Modern Britain* (London: Palgrave Macmillan, 1999).

MacGill, P., *Children of the Dead End* (Edinburgh: Birlinn, 1999).

MacGill, P., *The Navvy Poet* (London: Caliban Books, 1984).

Martin, R., *Oral History in Social Work* (California: Sage Publications, 1995).

Massie, S., *Irish History and Culture* (New York: Alfa, 1999).

McCaffrey, L.J., *The Irish Diaspora in America* (London: Indiana University Press, 1976).

McCracken, D.P., 'A Minority of Minority of a Minority: The Irish in South Africa, European Migrants', *Diasporas and Indigenous Ethnic Minorities*, 2008, pp. 157-73.

Meenan, J., *The Irish Economy Since 1922* (Liverpool: Liverpool University Press, 1970).

Meikle, J., 'Irish and Scots migrants more likely to die early', *The Guardian*, 25 October 2005.

Miller, K., *Emigrants and Exiles: Ireland and the Irish Exodus to North America* (New York: Oxford University Press, 1985).

Miller, K. et al., *Out of Ireland: The Story of Irish Emigration to America* (Washington DC: Elliott & Clark Publishing, 1994).

Mind, *Mental Health of Irish-born People in Britain* (London: Mind, 2001).

Montgomery, J., *The Fifties* (London: George Allen and Unwin, 1965).

Moya, J., 'Immigrants and Associations: A Global and Historical Perspective', *Journal of Ethnic and Migration Studies*, 31 (5), 2005, pp. 833-64.

Mullen, K.J., *Dangerous Strangers: Minority Newcomers and Criminal Violence in the Urban West, 1850-2000* (New York: Palgrave Macmillan, 2005).

Nasatir, A.P., *A French Journalist in the California Gold Rush: The Letters of Etienne Derbec* (Georgetown: The Talisman Press, 1964).

O'Brien, M., et al., *A Concise History of Ireland* (London: Thames and Hudson, 1972).

O'Callaghan, S., *To Hell or Barbados: The Ethnic Cleansing of Ireland* (Dublin: Brandon Books, 2001).

O'Connor, K., *The Irish in Britain* (Dublin: Torc Books, 1972).

O'Day, A., 'Revising the Diaspora' in Boyce, G. and O'Day, A. (eds), *The Making of Modern Irish History: Revisionism and the Revisionist Controversy* (London: Routledge, 1996).

O'Day, A. et al., *Irish Historical Documents Since 1800* (Dublin: Gill and Macmillan, 1992).

O'Dowd, A. et al. (eds), *Chattel, Servant or Citizen: Women's Status in Church, State and Society* (Belfast: The Institute of Irish Studies, 1995).

O'Farrell, P., *Ireland's English Question: Anglo-Irish Relations 1534-1970* (London: B.T. Batsford, 1971).

O'Gráda, C., *A rocky road: The Irish economy since the 1920s* (Manchester: Manchester University Press, 1997).

O'Keeffe, G., 'The Irish in Britain: Injustices of Recognition?', *Histoire, politique, éconimie, société,* Autumn 2003, pp. 33-43.

O'Leary, P., *Immigration and Integration: The Irish in Wales 1798-1922* (Cardiff: University of Wales Press, 2000).

O'Sullivan, P. (ed.), *Irish Women and Irish Migration* (London: Leicester University Press, 1997).

O'Toole, F., *The Irish Times: Book of the Century* (Dublin: Gill & Macmillan, 1999).

Planning and Research, *A History of the San Francisco Police Department* (San Francisco: research paper from the SF history center, 1972).

Peach, C., 'South Asian and Caribbean Ethnic Minority Housing Choice in Britain', *Urban Studies*, 35 (10), 1998, pp. 1657-80.

Peterson, N.S., *Raking the Ashes: Genealogical Strategies for Pre-1906 San Francisco Research* (Oakland: California Genealogical Society, 2011).

Porter, R., *London: A Social History* (London: Hamish Hamilton, 1994).

Power, A., *Hovels to High Rise: State Housing in Europe Since 1850* (London: Routledge, 1993).

Prendergast, F.T. *Forgotten Pioneers: Irish Leaders in Early California* (New York: Books for Libraries Press, 1942).

Pugh, M., *Britain Since 1789: A Concise History* (Houndmills: Macmillan Press, 1999).

Pugh, M., *State and Society: British Political & Social History 1870-1992* (London: Edward Arnold, 1994).

Radcliffe, Z., *London Irish (*London: Black Swan, 2002).

Reed, D., *Ireland: The Key to the British Revolution* (London: Larkin Publications, 1984).

Roberts, G., 'The Challenge of the Irish volunteers of World War II' in Keogh, D. et al. (eds), *Ireland and World War II* (Dublin: Mercier Press, 2004).

Roberts, G., 'Ireland's decision to sit out WWII is seen as a mistake on the 60th Anniversary of D-Day', *The Irish Times*, 24 June 2004.

Rogers, M., 'The London Session', *Rí–Rá*, 23 November 2004, p. 23.

Roney, F., *Irish Rebel and California Labor Leader: An Autobiography* (Berkeley: University of California Press, 1931).

Rossiter, A., 'Bringing the margins into the Centre: A review of aspects of Irish Women's Emigration' in Hutton, S. (ed.), et al., *Ireland's Histories: Aspects of State, Society and Ideology.* (London: Routledge, 1991).

Rouse, P., *Lost Generation* (London: TG4, 2003).

Royle, E., *Modern Britain: A Social History 1750-1985* (London: Edward Arnold, 1987).

Ryan, L., 'In the Green Fields of Kilburn: Reflections on a Quantitative Study of Irish Migrants in north London', *Anthropology Matters Journal*, 2003, pp. 1-6.

Ryan, L., 'Irish Emigration to Britain since World War Two' in Kearney, R. (ed.), *Migrations: The Irish at Home and Abroad* (Dublin: Wolfhound Press, 1990).

Ryan, L., 'Leaving Home: Irish Press Debates on Female Employment, Domesticity and Emigration to Britain in the 1930s', *Women's History Review*, 12 (3), 2003, pp. 387–406.

Ryan, L., 'Revisiting Ethnicity, Migration and Economy', *BSA Publications Ltd*, 38 (2), 2004, pp. 399–405.

Ryder, J. et al., *Modern English Society* (London: Methuen, 1970).

Salt, J. et al., *Migration in Post-war Europe* (London: Oxford University Press, 1976).

Schrier, A., *Ireland and the American Emigration 1850-1900* (Minneapolis: University of Minnesota Press, 1958).

Senkewicz, R.M., *Vigilantes in Gold Rush San Francisco* (Stanford: Stanford University Press, 1985).

Short, J.R., *Housing in Britain: The Post-war Experience* (London: Methuen, 1982).

Shufelt. S., *A Letter from a Gold Miner, Placerville, California, October 1850* (San Marino, Friends of the Huntington library, 1944).

Smith, Michael, *An Unsung Hero: Tom Crean – Antarctic Survivor* (Cork: The Collins Press, 2000).

Soule, F. et al., *The Annals of San Francisco and History of California* (Palo Alto: Lewis Osborne, 1966).

Standing, G., 'Conceptualising Territorial Mobility', *Migration Surveys in Low Income Countries: Guidelines for Survey and Questionnaire Design* (London: Croom Helm, 1984), pp. 31–59.

Stewart, G., *Committee of Vigilance: Revolution in San Francisco, 1851* (Boston: Houghton Mifflin Company, 1964).

Svejda, George, *Irish Immigrant Participation in the construction of the Erie Canal* (New York: Office of Archeology and Historic Preservation, 1966).

Sweeney, P., *The Irish Experience of Economic Lift Off* (Montreal: Bishops University, 2004).

Swift, R., *Irish Migrants in Britain, 1815-1914: Documentary History* (Cork: Cork University Press, 2002).

Swift, R., et al. (eds), *The Irish in the Victorian City* (London: Croom Helm, 1985).

TG4, *Damhsa an Deoraí – 50 years of the Galtymore* (London: TG4, 2002).

Thompson, E.P., *The Making of the English Working Class* (London: Penguin Books, 1963).

Toibin, C., et al., *The Irish Famine: A Documentary* (New York: Thomas Dunne Books, 2001).

Townshend, C., *The British Campaign in Ireland 1919-1921: The Development of Political and Military Policies* (Oxford: Oxford University Press, 1975).

Townshend, C., *Ireland the 20th Century* (London: Arnold, 1999).

Vigne, R., et al., *From Strangers to Citizens: The Integration of Immigrant Communities in Britain, Ireland and Colonial America, 1550-1750* (Sussex: Sussex Academic Press, 2001).

Waddington, H. et al., 'How does Poverty Affect Migration Choice?', *The Development Research Centre on Migration, Globalisation and Poverty Working Paper*, T3, 2003.

Walls, P., *Consulting the Irish Community on Inside Outside: Improving Mental Health Services for Black and Ethnic Minorities in England – the Community Response and its Evaluation* (London: The Federation of Irish Societies, 2003).

Walter, B., 'The Irish Community – diversity, disadvantage and discrimination', paper presented to the Commission on the Future of Multi-Ethnic Britain in 1999.

Walter, B. et al., *A Study of the Existing Sources of Information and Analysis about Irish Emigrants and Irish Communities Abroad* (Cambridge: Anglia Polytechnic University, 2002).

Walter, B., *Outsiders Inside: Whiteness, Place and Irish Women* (London: Routledge, 2000).

Webb, J., *Born Fighting, How the Scots-Irish Shaped America* (New York: Broadway Books, 2005).

Webster, W., *Imagining Home: Gender, Race and National Identity, 1945-64* (London: UCL Press, 1998).

Welch, P.A., *Thomas John Welsh Architect 1845-1918: A Journey of Discovery* (San Francisco: PAW Productions, 1993).

Welch, R. (ed.), *Concise companion to Irish Literature* (Oxford: Oxford University Press, 2000).

Wellman, D., *The Union Makes us Strong: Radical Unionism on the San Francisco Waterfront* (Cambridge: Cambridge University Press, 1995).

Whelan, K., *The Tree of Liberty, Radicalism, Catholicism and the Construction of Irish Identity 1760-1830* (Cork: Cork University Press, 1996).

White, P. et al. (eds), *The Geographical Impact of Migration* (London: Longman, 1980).

Whyte, Y.H., *Church and State in Modern Ireland 1923-1970* (Dublin: Gill and Macmillan, 1971).

Williamson, J.G., *Coping with City Growth During the British Industrial Revolution* (Cambridge: Cambridge University Press, 1990).

If you enjoyed this book, you may also be interested in…

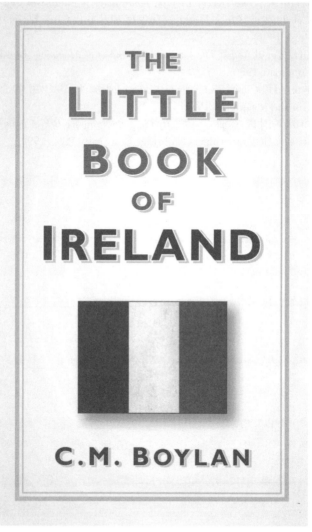

THE
LITTLE
BOOK
OF
IRELAND

C.M. BOYLAN

The Little Book of Ireland   978 1 84588 804 6

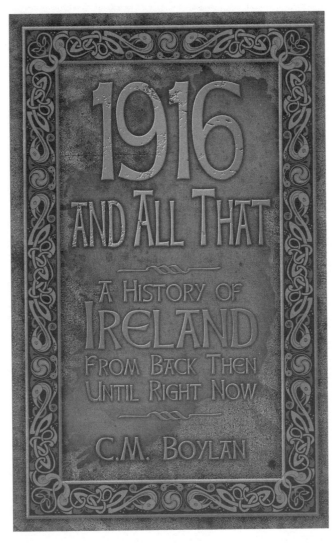

1916 and All That

978 1 84588 749 0

Visit our websites and discover thousands of other
History Press books.

www.thehistorypress.ie
www.thehistorypress.co.uk

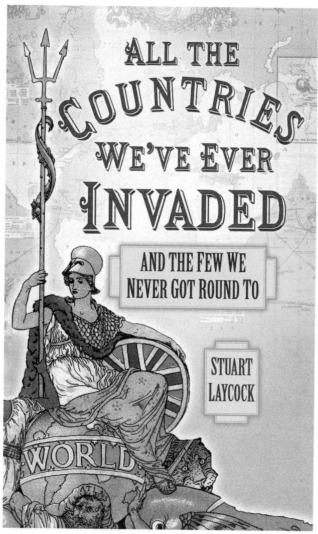

All the Countries We've Ever Invaded   978 0 7524 7969 9